Body of Clay
Soul of Fire

To: Joe & Kathy.
Thank you for so many years of
your care and support. Without your
kindness this would not have been
possible. You stood by me at the very
beginning and for your strength i will
be forever greatful. The touching note you
slipped into the door at home coming reached
into my heart that on a sunday you could take
the time to leave a potter a note of thanks.
Warmly,

11.07.01

Body of Clay
Soul of Fire

Richard Bresnahan and
the Saint John's Pottery

Matthew Welch

*With a Foreword
by Gerry Williams*

 Afton Historical Society Press

Publication of this book has been made possible by generous contributions from:

Saint John's Abbey and University
Target Corporation
Grotto Foundation
Jerome Foundation
Star Tribune Foundation
Marilynn and James Alcott
Patricia Blakely
Susan and Peter Brasket
Dr. Charles Burton
Anne and James Clark
Susan and Rob Culligan
Leigh Dillard and John Taylor
Jean and Bruce Freeman
Jane and Gregory Greene
Nina and Al Heckman

Arlene and Don Helgeson
Jane and Michael Kathman
Julia and Frank Ladner
Sara and David Lieberman
Nivin and W. Duncan MacMillan
Pamela McAlister and Gary Stoos
Elizabeth and William Nilles
JoAnn and James Nordlie
Jennifer Noyes and Franc Fennessy
Marilyn and Frank Rajkowski
Lois and John Rogers
Dr. Richard Shannon
Kristi Skordahl and J. Michael Dady
Sharon and Kenneth Voss
Margaret and Michael White

Cover: *Five-footed melon-shaped plate* (Johanna kiln, Tanegashima chamber), 1998, 10½ in. diameter
Photograph by Gary Mortensen

Frontispiece: Richard Bresnahan stoking the final chamber of the first kiln he built at Saint John's University
Photograph by James R. Dean, September 1990

Edited by Sandra L. Lipshultz
Designed by Barbara J. Arney

Library of Congress Cataloging-in-Publication Data
Welch, Matthew, 1958–
Body of clay, soul of fire: Richard Bresnahan and the Saint John's Pottery
by Matthew Welch; foreword by Gerry Williams.
p. cm.
Includes bibliograpical references.
ISBN -890434-45-0   ISBN -890434-46-9 (softcover)
1. Bresnahan, Richard, 1953– . 2. Potters—United States—Biography. I. Bresnahan, Richard.
II. Title.
NK4210.B694 W45 2001
738'.092—dc21

2001034079

The Afton Historical Society Press is a nonprofit organization that publishes
exceptional books on regional subjects.

W. Duncan MacMillan
President

Patricia Condon Johnston
Publisher

Afton Historical Society Press
P.O. Box 100
Afton, Minnesota 55001
1-800-436-8443
aftonpress@aftonpress.com

To the memory of
Father Michael Blecker,
Abbot Jerome Theisen,
and
Al Heckman,
who all believed in the
power of art
to cultivate the mind
and nourish the soul

Contents

Foreword 11

Acknowledgments 14

Chapter I
Taking Shape 19

Chapter II
A Stranger in a Strange Land 79

Chapter III
Body and Soul 109

Chapter IV
An Unlikely Teacher 143

Chapter V
The Artful Life 179

Appendices 215

  The Takigama Kiln 216

  The Johanna Kiln 218

  Ten-Day Firing Schedule 220

  Signature and Seals 224

  Exhibition History and Collections 225

  Apprentices and Visiting Artists 226

Selected Bibliography 228

Foreword

The story of Richard Bresnahan is one that entails a search for identity. Born on the windswept plains of Midwestern America, he apprenticed to a distinguished Japanese potter, who descended from Korean potters taken to Japan against their will. After returning to an academic monastic environment in Minnesota, Bresnahan is now making his way along the uncertain and sometimes baffling pathways of contemporary American ceramics. As with many of us, he has created a life that resulted from exposure to many influences.

The root of art in America is not so clearly defined as it is in some countries, where wholeness of process is nurtured by tradition, from both groups and communities. The uniqueness of contemporary American art comes, in part, from that absence of tradition, from the challenge to find inspiration in the arts of other cultures, transformed into new forms and spirit.

Yet there is an indigenous art that is wholly our own but little used. We need look no further than Mesoamerica to see major art forms at our doorstep. In Mexico, we find the Olmec, Maya, and Aztec, and farther south, the Moche, Nazca, and Inca—inheritances unused except by the Mimbres potters and the Pueblo Indians. Their ancient gods played prominent roles in aesthetic strategies. A Cochiti legend speaks of Old Clay Woman, who was sent from the *shipap*, or underworld, to teach the people how to make pots. Yet these traditions, too, were influenced or overturned by conquering cultures, both native and foreign, like the Spanish.

Most people think the story begins when Europeans discovered the American continent in the 15th century. At that time, the colonists imported forms and styles from England and Germany, as potters in the "wilderness" worked to supply wares for everyday use. English redware decorated by slip trailing and feathering became a staple in New England and the South and was widely made until German stoneware became more popular. These influences can still be seen today in traditional potteries throughout the Appalachian area.

Nineteenth-century American art potters looked to France and such Art Deco practitioners as George Ohr and Henry Varnum Poor. In late Victorian times, William Morris and the Arts and Crafts movement strongly influenced American potters, as did the German Bauhaus of the 1930s. At the same time, African influences appeared in traditional American potteries where indentured servants and craftspeople worked. The African imagery of face jugs, for example, became commonplace in the Southern Highlands, albeit without its connection to ancient African gods and ancestors.

Modern American ceramics continue to rely on the vessel as the primary form of expression. But a growing interest in Abstract Expressionism, with its psychological emphasis on the idea rather than the object, began to produce a new genre of idiosyncratic work. This can be seen in the art of Peter Voulkos, John Mason, and Paul Soldner, and continues today with the work of Kaneko Jun, Kenneth Price, and James Melchert. Nevertheless, while seemingly unconnected to traditional influences, their pieces also exhibit references to Zen philosophy and the role of chance in design, as well as to the notion of casual fluidity, found in the work of such sculptors as the Italian Carlo Zauli.

Simultaneously, influences also came from an opposite direction—the Far East. In the 1940s, the most significant authority for American potters was the English potter Bernard Leach. But early on, Leach had become enamored of Chinese pots from the Sung dynasty and later by the Japanese idea of *mingei*, an aesthetic based on the gospel of the Japanese writer and philosopher Yanagi Sōetsu and the potter Hamada Shōji. In turn, Leach traveled extensively in America, encouraging potters to search for sources of artistic inspiration and training in Japan and England. This reads like a modern legend: Old Clay Man Bernard Leach went from England to America to teach the natives how to make pottery. Thus, it seems, we continue to be inspired by godlike figures.

Many successful communications across international boundaries have occurred, between Americans learning from the Japanese and vice versa. Isamu Noguchi, born in this country of an American mother and a Japanese father, educated in both the United States and Japan, was profoundly inspired by traditional Japanese arts and values. Yet although Noguchi occasionally betrayed his sources, he always transformed his sculptures into something unique.

The history of contemporary ceramics is loaded with the names of American potters who have trained in Japan. These include Randy Johnston, who apprenticed with Shimaoka Tatsuzō in Mashiko; Donna Nicholas, who worked with Morino Hiroaki in Kyoto; Joy Brown, who studied with Morioka Shigeyoshi in Wakayama prefecture; Jeff Shapiro, who lived in Hamasaka and had Kabumoto Nobuo as his patron; Susanne and John Stephenson, who worked in Shigaraki; and Malcolm Wright, who apprenticed with Nakazato Takashi in Karatsu. Deeply affected by their Japanese experiences, these artists have written extensively about them.

Japanese potters also have come to the United States, often because of their stated desire to escape tradition and work with greater freedom. Morino Hiroaki went to the University of Chicago; Kajitani Ban, to Utah State University; Yanagihara Mutsuo, to the University of Washington and Scripps College in California; and Takamori Akio, to the Kansas City Art Institute. Some, disillusioned with America, returned to Japan, while others have remained here, becoming prominent ceramists on the American scene.

Richard Bresnahan's training in Japan came about through serendipity. He studied with the distinguished art historian Sister Johanna Becker, and it was she who obtained his apprenticeship with Nakazato Takashi in Karatsu. I first met Takashi in Vermont at the home of Malcolm Wright and then visited him in Japan in 1996. A soft-spoken, gracious person, Takashi showed me through an exhibition of his work and around the Karatsu pottery. That the young Richard Bresnahan lived and worked in such an environment—rich in tradition, technique, and Japanese culture—makes him a very fortunate man indeed.

In 1993 and 1994, Bresnahan built a massive wood-burning kiln in Minnesota, which he named Johanna after his mentor. The very size of the large kiln, with its innovative flame flues and water channels, dwarfs all other American kilns and presents a challenge for other potters interested in wood firing. Building the kiln within a dedicated religious and academic environment also gives Bresnahan the opportunity to offer apprenticeships and promote community outreach. His detailed research into using local seeds and hulls as glazing materials supports the idea of ecological conservation and diminishes the dependence on industrial chemicals.

Bresnahan's pots are lovingly fashioned and in a great variety of shapes. He creates both traditional and nontraditional forms—covered jars, bowls, pitchers, ewers, urns, platters, vases, and teapots—all splendidly designed and enhanced by the wood ash deposited on them during the firing. This marriage of art and technique, the result of long training in making and firing, has also led Bresnahan to develop an intimate appreciation for natural colors and textures. His art clearly falls within the rich tradition of American pottery, for his style is at once simple and profound. Like another Saint John's artist, the renowned novelist J. F. Powers, whose clear prose belies the effort that went into its making, Bresnahan creates pots that are deceptively natural and unpretentious but with a discernible air of great accomplishment.

At the 1999 International Woodfire Conference in Iowa City, I gave a lecture entitled "Gifts of Fire: Gods, Heroes, and Icons." In discussing the mythology of fire in different cultures, I talked about gods that Joseph Campbell referred to as "Lords of Death and Resurrection." Such gods give meaning and energy to wood-firing potters. In Greek mythology, for example, Prometheus made men out of clay and stole fire from heaven to give to them. Vulcan, the Roman god of fire, has long been associated with pottery and metalmaking. Blacksmith to the gods, Vulcan also taught humankind the proper use of fire, while his assistants—the Cyclopes—forged lightning bolts that they hurled down onto the earth. The Phoenix, a fabulous and miraculous bird, lived five hundred years or more. When its time had come, it made a nest of twigs, sat on it, and then burned itself alive by setting the nest on fire. From the fragrant ashes arose a new young Phoenix. Thus, the theme of death and resurrection through fire became inextricably linked.

Today, such mythic personalities might be referred to as icons—individuals deserving of special attention and commendation. Such leaders stand out above the rest and can be identified by their unique vision, singular knowledge, or stylistic influence. One of these leaders is Richard Bresnahan. His 87-foot-long, wood-burning kiln is the largest in America and its 37-foot-long, back-pressure tunnel is widely acknowledged as the first of its design. Potters from near and far participate in his firings, which also become community events. In this way, information about the modern use of this ancient art is spread and interest in pottery making generated. As both an artist and an ambassador for the natural environment, Bresnahan takes his place as one of the preeminent potters in contemporary American ceramics.

Gerry Williams
Editor of *Studio Potter*
Goffstown, New Hampshire
March 6, 2001

Acknowledgments

Art historians like the order and logic that temporal distance brings to the study of an artist's life and work. The "messiness" of dealing with living artists, who often have difficulty explaining their creations while bemoaning the attempts of others to do so, has prompted more than one of us to declare, "The deader, the better!" It was, therefore, with some trepidation that I organized an exhibition of Richard Bresnahan's ceramics in 1996 for The Minneapolis Institute of Arts and, later, agreed to write this book about him and the Saint John's Pottery. But throughout the lengthy process of gathering information for both projects, I encountered a person who answered my countless questions with remarkable clarity and insight into both his professional and personal life. I also brushed shoulders with an individual of uncommon integrity, grace, energy, and good humor. For such a rare and wondrous opportunity, I will be forever thankful to Richard Bresnahan.

I also am indebted to Sister Johanna Becker at the College of Saint Benedict for having recommended me as the author of this book. As Bresnahan's mentor, she provided important information about his early development as a potter. And as a specialist in Japanese ceramics, she offered valuable advice at the early stages of preparing the manuscript.

I appreciate the astonishing kindness of many people at Saint John's Abbey and University. Brother Dietrich Reinhart, the university's current president, indulged me with two morning-long interviews. Brother Gregory

Potter Richard Bresnahan (front) and author Matthew Welch worked together for three years to create this book. Photograph by James R. Dean, November 2000.

Eibensteiner, Brother Dennis Beach, Father Paul Schweitz, and Father Jerome Tupa all patiently and thoroughly answered my questions about Bresnahan, the pottery, and the history of their Benedictine community. Father Daniel Durken of Saint John's Liturgical Press carefully reviewed portions of the manuscript and made many helpful suggestions, and Brother David Klingeman gave me information about Saint John's Abbey and photographs from its archives. In addition, I owe an enormous debt to Rob Culligan and John Taylor in the Offices of Institutional Advancement for their unwavering faith in this undertaking and their heroic efforts in securing funding for it. John Taylor also generously read the entire manuscript. His unfailing enthusiasm and quick wit helped me through many dark moments over the past three years.

I thank Gerry Williams, cofounder and editor of *Studio Potter*, for graciously agreeing to provide the book's foreword. In his mid-seventies, Williams has had his finger on the pulse of American ceramics longer than most other potters have been alive. He deftly explained the history of American ceramics and the unique contribution that Richard Bresnahan has made to that enduring tradition.

Special recognition also goes to James R. Dean, architect and photographer extraordinaire. Over the past twenty years, he has taken thousands of black-and-white images of Bresnahan, both at the studio and with his family, and of the pottery's many apprentices and visiting artists. Dean's archive, meticulously labeled and numbered, proved to be an invaluable resource for this project, and his unpretentious but compelling "snapshots" have become an integral part of this book. I also am indebted to him for his thoughtful advice, steadfastness, and friendship.

That so many of Bresnahan's past apprentices and artist-colleagues have been willing to share their thoughts and feelings about him with me testifies to his stature within the creative community. My gratitude goes to all those who completed my lengthy questionnaire and answered my unexpected phone calls. Their unique perspectives have helped me to understand Bresnahan, the teacher. I am thankful, too, for Jean Matske's dogged determination in tracking down "missing" artists who have had residencies at the pottery and for securing permission to publish their works.

I am deeply beholden to two remarkable women, Colette Bresnahan and Michelle Welch, who ably shouldered more than their fair share of family responsibilities while their husbands labored over this book. Without their help and understanding, it never would have reached completion. And without their loving support over the years, it is doubtful that either Richard or I could have achieved the modest success we now enjoy.

In helping to produce this book, I thank Gary Mortensen and Robert Fogt for their outstanding color photographs of the objects included. I also acknowledge Patricia Johnston of Afton Historical Society Press for overseeing the printing of the book and Barbara Arney for bringing the myriad elements together into an elegantly designed whole.

A final thank-you goes to my editor Sandra Lipshultz, a colleague of mine at The Minneapolis Institute of Arts, with whom I have worked on numerous projects. She offered many valuable suggestions during the conceptual planning of the book and faithfully shepherded it through completion, from the initial edit to the last page proofs. A passionate advocate for the reader, she kept the twin demons of Verbosity and Disorder at bay, rendering my text infinitely more coherent and eloquent. For her unerring judgment and keen intelligence, we can all rejoice.

Matthew Welch
Minneapolis, Minnesota
May 18, 2001

Notes to the Reader

Unless otherwise noted, Richard Bresnahan made all the works illustrated in this book.

In the text, Japanese names have been written in Japanese style, with the surname first and the given name second. Upon first mention, an individual's full name is cited. Thereafter, only the surname is used. However, when several members of the same family are discussed, the given name is used after the first reference to avoid confusion.

Because of Bresnahan's association with Saint John's Abbey and the Monastery of Saint Benedict, which are both Benedictine communities, the reader should assume that all the monastic men and women discussed in the text belong to the Order of Saint Benedict. Upon first mention, their full names are given, along with their religious titles (brother, sister, father, abbot, and so on). Thereafter, as is customary within such orders, their given names are used with their titles.

A shortened reference style has been used in the text. Full citations for these printed sources can be found in the bibliography. A great deal of information also came through personal interviews conducted over the past three years. As unpublished communications, these sources have not been listed in the bibliography, nor have Bresnahan's personal journals, which provided background material for his apprenticeship in Japan.

Taking Shape

He lay face up in the grassy ditch, fighting to remain conscious, his left leg snapped in two. Moments earlier, he had been driving a borrowed motorcycle to work when the throttle cable locked in place. The bike careened out of control toward a row of parked cars, and as he felt the pavement tearing at his right pant leg, his left thigh hit the last car's bumper.

It was May 3, 1979, and the 25-year-old man was Richard Bresnahan. An ambulance rushed him to St. Alexius Hospital in Bismarck, North Dakota. For the next six weeks he would be confined to bed, his broken leg pinned and elevated in traction. What could have been a terrible calamity for the young man proved to be a catharsis. After the initial flurry of visits from family and friends, Bresnahan settled into the quiet routine of hospital life. The television that hung from the ceiling of his room remained dark. And as he stared out the window and across the vast prairie toward the Missouri River, he began to review his past and decide his future.

Gourd-shaped teapot (Johanna kiln, front fire chamber), 1995, stoneware with iron slip, 6 3/4 in. high. Reed handle by Paul Krueger. Dried gourds have long been used in Asia to decant water and wine. During pouring, the unusual shape creates a pleasant gurgling sound.
Photograph by Gary Mortensen.

Opposite page: Bresnahan uses a Karatsu-style kick wheel and throws "off the hump" in the Japanese manner.
Photograph by James R. Dean, 1996.

19

Striped cups **(Johanna kiln, Tanegashima chamber), 1995, stoneware with clay-slip painting, 5½ in. high (each).**
Photograph by Gary Mortensen.

Six months earlier he had returned home after spending three-and-a-half years in Japan, where he had apprenticed under a master potter on the island of Kyushu. Since then, he had been offered teaching positions at Georgetown University in Washington, D.C., and the College of Marin in Kentfield, California. And Saint John's University in Collegeville, Minnesota, had promised him an appointment as artist-in-residence. But Bresnahan felt unsettled, plagued with questions about how to apply his Japanese experience to his life in America. He thought about the kind of studio he wanted to build and the philosophy he would follow to operate it. He wondered about his own evolution as an artist and how to make his pottery reflect both his Japanese training and his Midwestern roots. Holding down three part-time jobs that spring had left him exhausted and with little chance for reflection. But now, lying peacefully against the crisp hospital sheets, he finally had the luxury of time—time to think and to plan.

Left to right: Bresnahan, Howard Brown, and Kevin Flicker near a kaolin deposit at the Meridian Aggregate Company in Waite Park, Minnesota.
Photograph by James R. Dean, June 1987.

The rolling farmlands and vast skies of North Dakota frequently appear in Bresnahan's slip-painted bowls and platters.
Photograph by Todd Hunter Strand, 1976.

The Early Years

Born on July 4, 1953, in Fargo, North Dakota, Richard John Bresnahan II grew up nearby in Casselton, one of many small farming communities in the fertile Red River Valley. His father ran a modest grain-elevator company, and his mother cared for the six Bresnahan children. In a town with only a thousand residents, the Bresnahans knew nearly everybody. Thirty-two cousins lived in the area, and the 5,120-acre Sinner-Bresnahan farm, which Richard's uncles and cousins ran, was one mile east of town.

By all accounts, Casselton was a safe and wholesome place for children. Within minutes of leaving his house, Bresnahan could disappear into the cornfields. He roamed far and wide, following creeks that dried up by mid-July. In summer, he fished and swam in the local reservoir, and every Sunday, he went golfing with his father. The entire Bresnahan clan gathered at the farm to celebrate birthdays and holidays, staging grand picnics followed by softball games. In winter, they skated on frozen ponds and delighted in being pulled through snow drifts on a toboggan attached to the bumper of the family station wagon.

Iris platter (Johanna kiln, glaze chamber), 1995, stoneware with white slip and iron painting under a basswood ash glaze, 15 in. diameter.
Photograph by Gary Mortensen.

Spice jars (Johanna kiln, Tanegashima chamber), 1995, stoneware, 5 in. high (each).
Photograph by Gary Mortensen.

Despite its rural location, Casselton had an East Coast gentility about it. Many of the town's sons and daughters had gone to Ivy League schools, and four had become governors of North Dakota. Bresnahan's paternal grandmother, Phila Adelaide, who had arrived in Casselton in 1915 at the age of 22 from York, Nebraska, understood the value of a good education and proper deportment. To ensure that her grandchildren acquired the social graces, she hosted mandatory tea parties, teaching them etiquette and

Five-footed melon-shaped plate (Johanna kiln, Tanegashima chamber), 1998, stoneware, 10 ½ in. diameter. Bresnahan created the circular markings on this plate by setting three inverted cups on it during the loading process. Wild rice hulls, heaped around the vessels, caused the slight iridescence.
Photograph by Gary Mortensen.

serving cakes and Darjeeling using her finest blue-and-white porcelain. And for those children who seemed receptive, she revealed the world beyond North Dakota's farms. "Isn't this a beautiful place?" she would ask young Richard as they looked at *National Geographic* magazines together. "Wouldn't you like to go there?" An amateur painter herself who copied the works of famous artists, she was the first person to encourage Bresnahan to draw.

Despite his happy childhood, Bresnahan had a troubled adolescence. Bright and good-natured, he was well liked by teachers and classmates alike. But he had difficulty reading, and as his schoolwork became increasingly demanding, he became more frustrated and dispirited. His parents, realizing the local public school could not solve their son's learning problems, decided to send him to Saint John's Preparatory School in Collegeville, Minnesota. Bresnahan's father had attended Saint John's University in the late 1940s, and Bresnahan himself had gone to week-long leadership camps there during the summers of 1966 and 1967.

Founded in 1856, Saint John's Preparatory School and University are both part of a sprawling Benedictine monastery in central Minnesota. Situated on 2,500 acres of lakes, grasslands, and forests, the campus itself wraps around the north side of Lake Sagatagan. While leaving his family proved difficult, 14-year-old Bresnahan was excited about going away to school and impressed with Saint John's traditional red-brick buildings and avant-garde church and bell tower. And while the monks appeared formidable in their dark robes, they also were devoted and kind teachers. Many, in fact, became idols to their young charges. Father Otto Weber, for example, taught Latin and theology and as a former all-American wrestler often demonstrated the finer points of pinning opponents; Father Daniel Ward assigned such reading as Hermann Hesse's *Siddhartha* and *Narcissus and Goldmund* and then challenged the class to confront their own thoughts and feelings about existence.

Saint John's idyllic setting and nurturing teachers soon had a positive effect on Bresnahan. Although he still struggled with his studies—and would throughout high school and college—he received the help he needed. Life on a university campus also exposed the North Dakota farm boy to the most pressing social and political issues of the late 1960s and early 1970s. Under Lyndon B. Johnson's ABC (A Better Chance) Program, inner-city youths were enrolled in private institutions like Saint John's. As Bresnahan watched them falter, he became aware of the devastating effects of urban poverty and hopelessness. He also came face-to-face with the victims of America's drug culture, meeting wealthy addicted kids who had been sent to the school in an attempt to save them.

At the same time, Bresnahan attended rousing speeches by some of the most controversial and brilliant thinkers of the day. The Catholic priests Daniel and Philip Berrigan visited the campus, advocating resistance to nuclear armament and vehemently criticizing the U.S. government's conscription policies for the Vietnam War.

Small bottle (Johanna kiln, Tanegashima chamber), 1998, stoneware, 9 3/8 in. high. Bresnahan made the dramatic color shifts on the shoulder of this bottle by inverting it into a cup partially filled with seashells. During firing, the seashells produced the salt glaze on the pot's mouth and neck.
Photograph by Gary Mortensen.

Dorothy Day, founder of the Catholic Worker movement, spoke about the plight of common laborers and the unemployed destitute. Mathematician Buckminster Fuller, inventor of the geodesic dome, talked about his concern for humankind's future in light of vanishing natural resources.

Within this atmosphere, Bresnahan became increasingly politicized. Soon, he was protesting against nuclear armament and demonstrating against the war in Vietnam. And when he applied for admission to Saint John's University for the fall of 1972, he wrote that his intended major would be political science. As a government advisor or policy maker, he reasoned, he could affect change and help build a better society.

Spice jar (Johanna kiln, front fire chamber), 1997, stoneware with natural ash glaze, 5 in. high.
Photograph by Gary Mortensen.

Student Days

To balance the heavy demands of class work in government and social policy, Bresnahan enrolled in a studio art course at the neighboring College of Saint Benedict in St. Joseph, Minnesota. (Saint John's and the college share a common curriculum with identical degree requirements, which allows students to take classes on both campuses.) He chose ceramics with Bill Smith, who had completed a master of fine arts degree at Mills College in Oakland, California. Although Smith produced finely crafted porcelain vases with subtle celadon glazes, he began the semester by discussing the work of other artists. Encouraging his students to experiment, he showed them utilitarian wares and contemporary sculpture, urging them to discover for themselves the breadth of clay's artistic potential.

The course was unlike anything Bresnahan had ever experienced before. After being away from the farm in North Dakota for four years, he liked using his hands again. He also felt liberated working without a rigidly prescribed objective, and he seemed to have an affinity for the potter's wheel. After years of trying to keep

Teapot **(Johanna kiln, Tanegashima chamber), 1998, stoneware with natural ash glaze, 6 3/4 in. high.**
Photograph by Gary Mortensen.

up in academic classes, he had finally found something that came naturally to him. When the semester ended, he re-enrolled, and by the end of his freshman year, he was focused in a way that was unique for him and becoming interested in a career in the arts.

During the summer of 1973, Smith invited Bresnahan and a few other students to go with him to Banff for the first international conference on ceramics to be held in North America. Sponsored by the Canadian government and the province of Alberta, the proceedings took on the air of a world summit meeting. Upon arrival, participants received headsets so they could listen to the talks in English, French, or German. Over the next five days, luminaries in contemporary ceramics gave presentations and demonstrations. Michael Cardew introduced a Nigerian potter who constructed traditional coil-and-paddle jars and used pit firings. Amid cheers and heckling, Peter Voulkos reviewed ceramics by California's Funk artists. Dennis Parks explained how to build a kiln fueled by discarded motor oil; Ruth Duckworth spoke about the effects of multiple firings. And in nearby Calgary, a large juried exhibition of pottery was on view.

All told, the event proved revelatory for Bresnahan. Since most of the speakers made their livelihoods from ceramics, they talked with passion and conviction about their art. They also discussed modern industrialization and its negative impact on the earth's ecosystems. Reiterating the sentiments of William Morris and the Arts and Crafts movement, they lamented the loss of handmade objects from people's daily lives and reviled the widespread use of mass-produced ceramics and plastics.

Tall bottle with three lugs **(Johanna kiln, front fire chamber), 1997, stoneware with natural ash glaze, 15 1/8 in. high.**
Photograph by Gary Mortensen.

Jar (Johanna kiln, front fire chamber), 1999, stoneware with paddled decor and natural ash glaze, 19 1/2 in. high.
Photograph by Gary Mortensen.

Vase (Johanna kiln, front fire chamber), 1995, stoneware with slip painting and natural ash glaze, 13 3/4 in. high. Photograph by Gary Mortensen.

"I don't remember him as a student I had to stimulate," she said, "but someone I had to keep drawing back to something that was more workable and functional."

That same fall Smith hired him for a work-study job in Saint Benedict's ceramic studio. There, Bresnahan mixed glazes, wedged clay, and cleaned the kiln. He got up early every day to spend a few hours in the studio before going to classes. After dinner, he returned and worked late into the night. In the spring of 1974, he officially changed his major from political science to fine arts, with an emphasis in ceramics.

In addition to Smith, Sister Johanna Becker greatly influenced Bresnahan during his college years. A professed member of Saint Benedict's Monastery and a professor at the college there, Sister Johanna was trained as a potter. She had received a master of fine arts degree from Ohio State University and was completing a doctorate in Japanese art history from the University of Michigan when Bresnahan first met her.

After the conference, Bresnahan returned to North Dakota for summer break, excited and energized. With what little money he had, he bought an electric wheel and clay and threw pots in every spare moment. When he returned to Saint John's that fall, he had a truckload of wares ready to be fired. Sister Johanna Becker, from whom Bresnahan had taken Asian ceramic classes, recalled that he arrived with a "super-abundance of things" and was "dynamic, enthusiastic, and full of ideas that were ambitious beyond reality."

Small bottle (Johanna kiln, front fire chamber), 1997, stoneware with natural ash glaze, 6 1/4 in. high. Photograph by Gary Mortensen.

Large jar (Johanna kiln, front fire chamber), 1997, stoneware with paddled decor and natural ash glaze, 32 in. high.

Photograph by Gary Mortensen.

Her knowledge and intuitive understanding of Asian ceramics so impressed Bresnahan that he took every course she offered at Saint Benedict's and regularly sought out her opinion about his pottery.

Sister Johanna's dissertation focused on Japanese Karatsu ware, a type of stoneware first produced in the late 16th century by émigré Korean potters in northwest Kyushu. Known for its simple iron-brown decorations and subtle monochromatic glazes, Karatsu ware became a favorite with Japanese tea masters during the Edo period (1600–1868) because of its humble nature. Sister Johanna had been invited by Koyama Fujio, Japan's foremost ceramic historian and an accomplished potter, to conduct research at the Idemitsu Museum of Arts in Tokyo. He and Etō Takashi, the museum's curatorial manager, had, in turn, introduced her to the Nakazatos, a family of potters who had been making Karatsu ware for thirteen generations.

In particular, Sister Johanna met Nakazato Tarōuemon XII, who would later become a "Living National Treasure," and his son Tadao, who had just succeeded his father as head

Teacups (Johanna kiln, glaze chamber), 1998, stoneware with white slip and iron painting under a flax-straw ash glaze, 4 1/4 in. high (left), 4 in. high (right).
Photograph by Gary Mortensen.

of the Nakazato studio, taking the name Tarōuemon XIII. But it was with Takashi, Tarōuemon's fifth son, that she spent most of her time in Japan. He took her to various old kiln sites in Karatsu, telling her about local clays and how different firing techniques affected specific Karatsu wares.

Widely recognized as one of Japan's preeminent ceramic throwers, Takashi had trained in his father's studio and at the Kyoto Ceramic Institute and the Saga Prefecture Ceramic Research Institute in Saga City. After traveling to the United States in 1967 to lecture and give demonstrations and then touring Europe, the Middle East, Thailand, and Korea to learn more about other ceramic traditions, he worked at Ochawangama, the family kiln in Karatsu. In 1971, he built a kiln on Tanegashima, a small island off the southern coast of Kyushu, where he lived for the next three years. In 1974, he returned to Karatsu to establish his own permanent studio.

Not surprisingly, when Bresnahan went to Sister Johanna at the end of his junior year for advice about his future, she thought of Takashi. Saint John's had a program that allowed students to spend a semester of their senior year abroad. Japan had one of the most active and innovative pottery traditions in the world. Sister Johanna reasoned that Bresnahan could benefit enormously by learning the self-sufficient pottery methods practiced by the

Tripod vase with ears (Johanna kiln, front fire chamber), 1997, stoneware with natural ash glaze, 9 1/4 in. high.
Photograph by Gary Mortensen.

Japanese, and she promised to make inquiries on his behalf during her next trip there.

After classes ended, Bresnahan returned to North Dakota, excited about the prospect of studying in Asia. To earn enough money for a plane ticket and other expenses, he waited on tables and drove a bread delivery truck. At night, he worked as a security guard. In what little free time he had, he read the few books he could find on Japanese ceramics in English.

But by midsummer, he still had not heard from Sister Johanna. He had begun to lose hope when suddenly a postcard arrived from Japan. The short message in her tidy script read: "Apprenticeship secured. Get passport ready."

Tea bowl (Johanna kiln, Tanegashima chamber), 1995, stoneware, 3½ in. high. The generous proportions and slightly flared mouths of 15th- and 16th-century Korean rice bowls inspired this design. The pale saffron color found here is extremely rare and occurred on only three of the 8,000 pieces from the Johanna kiln's first firing.
Photograph by Gary Mortensen.

Canisters (Johanna kiln, front fire chamber), 1998, stoneware with white slip and iron painting, 12 ¾ in. high (each).
Photograph by Gary Mortensen.

The construction of Nakazato Takashi's studio, located near the port city of Karatsu on the island of Kyushu.
August 1975.

The Apprenticeship in Japan

Knowing very little Japanese, Bresnahan arrived in Tokyo on August 18, 1975, and five days later departed for the southern island of Kyushu and Takashi's studio. Located in a heavily forested mountain valley five miles outside the port city of Karatsu, the compound consisted of a studio, an apprentices' lodge, and a building for clay storage and processing. (Takashi's own house had not been constructed yet, and he lived in Karatsu with his wife and three young children.) A boulder near the studio's entrance was engraved with three ideograms calling it "Ryūtagama." Later, Bresnahan learned that "ryū" is an alternate reading for "Takashi," and "ta" comes from the first character of Takashi's father's name, Tarōuemon. Both characters also signify prosperity, making the name suitably auspicious.

The studio itself had four traditional kick wheels and a forty-cubic-foot, double-car gas kiln. A shed roof had been erected over a nearby hillside, where the wood-burning kiln would later be built. All the buildings, in traditional Japanese style, had massive wooden beams, post-and-lintel supports, and fine clay walls. Although the carpenters still had finishing work to do, Bresnahan could not have imagined a better situation. "I am in a place of excellence, peace, and earthiness," he wrote in his journal, with "an unbelievable knowledge of clay."

Foliate bowl (Johanna kiln, glaze chamber), 1995, stoneware with navy-bean straw ash glaze, 5 7/8 in. high. Streaks of shimmering blue cascade toward the inside bottom of this elegant bowl. Bresnahan creates this subtle glaze by mixing navy-bean straw ash, from his family's farm in Casselton, North Dakota, with feldspar and clay. Photograph by Gary Mortensen.

But Bresnahan would not meet Takashi until a month later. Koyama Fujio had died the day Bresnahan arrived in Karatsu, and Takashi had quickly left to help Koyama's family in Minō. For Bresnahan, however, work began immediately, and as was typical of a Japanese apprenticeship, he was assigned the most menial tasks. Senior apprentices Noguchi, Kimura, and Ōoka had him cleaning the studio, hauling clay, and wedging it, dividing it into three-pound balls ready for throwing. He carried boards and pottery bats to the river and stood in knee-high water to clean them. Only after demonstrating his familiarity with handling pots was he allowed to wash their feet in preparation for firing.

He also received instruction on how to operate the stamper, a machine that pulverized bits of dried clay (leftover from trimming the pots) and crushed raw clay rich in iron deposits. After sifting the powder, he remoistened it and ran it through a pug mill to ensure an even consistency and remove any trapped air

bubbles. After several weeks at the studio, he was taught how to make glazes by dissolving ash in water and then screening the mixture to remove any impurities. And eventually, under the watchful eye of Kimura, he learned how to apply glazes rapidly and evenly by dipping greenware into a vat of feldspathic solution. (It was not unusual, for example, for Bresnahan to glaze two to three hundred bowls a day for gas firings.)

Over time, Bresnahan developed a routine. He would rise by 7 A.M. and make a fire in the *irori*, an open hearth used for heating and cooking. As the studio warmed up, he would eat breakfast before cleaning the kick wheels and carrying buckets of trimmings to the stamper in the clay storage building. If more glazes needed to be made, he would grind ash in the pot mill. By mid-morning when the other potters began arriving, he would be back in the studio, wedging clay and taking the boards holding their freshly thrown pots to the drying racks. In the afternoons, he was often sent on errands. He ate dinner with Takashi and the other apprentices around 6 P.M. and then relaxed for awhile in the *furo* (a hot, deep Japanese bath). Often, they would return to the studio in the evening and work until 11 P.M., and while the others threw pots, Bresnahan would wedge more clay and carry more boards.

Toward the end of October, everyone from the studio traveled to Minō to assist with the firing of Koyama Fujio's last works. Despite his lack of experience with wood-burning kilns, Bresnahan was warmly welcomed by the other potters. He was doubly honored when they asked him to help stoke the kiln, a procedure that would last seven days in eight-hour shifts. As he met the illustrious potters there, including Koyama Shin'ichi, Koyama Fujio's son; Arakawa Toyozō, a "Living National Treasure"; and Tsukamoto Kaiji, Bresnahan began to understand Takashi's status in Japan and his own privileged position as his apprentice.

Another revelation came when the kiln was opened. The stoking area was unbricked first, and when Bresnahan looked inside, he was stunned. A heavy ash covered everything, and the loading appeared chaotic, with cups and bowls wedged between larger vessels. (He was used to the clean heat of gas and electric kilns, and the regular, orderly spacing of the pieces to ensure an even firing.) He also was surprised by the seriousness with which the unloading took place. For with an exactitude that resembled archaeology, the potters carefully removed each layer of works,

taking photographs of their position in the kiln and then arranging them in rows on the ground for further cataloguing. Later, when Bresnahan helped wash the pots, he made his next discovery—the pieces were unglazed. The subtle earthen colors and soft tactile surfaces had been produced naturally, through the firing process alone.

A few weeks after Takashi's group returned to Karatsu, construction of the wood-burning kiln there began. It was early December, cold and damp, and altogether the process would take five months. But the experience would prove to be one of Bresnahan's most formative in Japan—and one of the most physically challenging.

Takashi's design for the kiln was as ambitious as it was innovative. The six-chamber structure was to be a hybrid of several kiln types. The front chamber, or firebox, was to be topped by a semispherical *manjū* arch. The next three chambers, for glazed pottery, were to be a traditional Karatsu-style *noborigama*, a climbing kiln rising fifteen degrees up the hillside with the interior walls pierced by flues at ground level. The fifth chamber, inspired by Takashi's time on Tanegashima island, was to be an elongated *teppogama*, a rifle-style kiln that was stoked from above through portals on either side of the arch. It was to be twelve feet long and would hold unglazed wares. The final chamber, reserved for salt glazes, would be only four feet long and continue the seven-degree slope of the previous three chambers.

Such an amalgam of kiln types had never been attempted before in Japan and reveals Takashi's astonishing willingness to experiment and improvise. In Asia, potters loyally duplicate regional kiln structures generation after generation. For Bresnahan, the chance to build a kiln capable of producing such a range of wares was exhilarating. "Each apprentice was given a photocopy of the design and dimensions," he wrote in his journal. "It will be a three-chamber *noborigama*, a fourth chamber *teppogama*, and a salt kiln. I don't have to go anywhere else to learn of kilns—this is it all in one!"

Over the next four months, Bresnahan would be involved in nearly every aspect of the kiln's construction. For days on end, he dug the hillside, preparing it for the *noborigama*'s stepped foundation and flue tunnel. Then, he hauled truckloads of brick,

most used previously in other Nakazato family kilns, and spent countless hours chipping old mortar off the blocks. "I have blisters under my calluses," he wrote at the time, but in the process he learned how to spot bad brick. "When it turns porous and white, as though oxidized by hundreds of firings, it will crumble under the edge of the hammer."

He also learned how to lay brick and build arches—often by trial and error. After Takashi finished the arched doorway into the first glaze chamber, he told Bresnahan to build the remaining arches. Lacking practice, Bresnahan spent the next several days completing the five doorways. But after inspecting them, Takashi told him the brickwork was unstable. "The rise exceeded the rise-span relationship," Bresnahan wrote in January of 1976. "So I had to tear down what I thought was perfect and rebuild them."

Bresnahan finishing the exterior arch of Nakazato Takashi's kiln with a layer of clay and straw.
April 1976.

He also gained expertise at recognizing different grades of mortar, depending on the insulating value needed, and at working with castable refractory materials. Little known in the United States at that time, such mortars were used in areas, like stoking portals, where the forms needed to be reasonably precise and heat resistant at the same time. In addition, Bresnahan was taught how to insulate brick by coating it with a two-inch mixture of chopped straw and clay. Furthermore, he learned how to make a waterproof mortar by combining lime with clay, which was applied to places that were susceptible to water damage, like the flue tunnel.

Kinuta-shaped vase **(Johanna kiln, glaze chamber), 1995, stoneware with navy-bean straw ash glaze, 12 in. high. The shape of this vase derives from the round wooden mallets used in China and Japan to soften newly woven silk. The glaze Bresnahan applied to the mouth and shoulder of this vessel spilled down the dark brown body of the pot in glossy cascades of white and blue.**
Photograph by Gary Mortensen.

Spouted jars **(Johanna kiln, front fire chamber), 1999, stoneware with natural ash glaze, 4 1/4 in. high (each).**
Photograph by Gary Mortensen.

Large jar (Johanna kiln, glaze chamber), 1995, coiled-and-paddled stoneware with navy-bean straw ash glaze and natural ash glaze, 18 in. high.

Photograph by Gary Mortensen.

At the same time, Takashi's unconventional personality made him receptive to his foreign apprentice's suggestions. For instance, when Bresnahan realized that flames and sparks from the kiln's chimney created a potential fire hazard—an age-old problem for Japanese potters—he proposed capping it with a catenary arch, which would split the flame and thus limit its projectile. Takashi's willingness to adopt this modification taught Bresnahan the value of trying his own building designs and not slavishly imitating traditional solutions.

While the kiln construction was underway, it was also necessary to keep the studio running. Bresnahan not only carried out his menial duties there, but he also started throwing his own pots in early January 1976. Although skilled at using an electric wheel, Bresnahan found the traditional Karatsu wheel, with its small twelve-inch kick wheel, difficult to control, especially in his Japanese-style socks. "I never felt so uncoordinated," he wrote, "as when *sensei* [teacher] started giving me lessons on the wheel for the first time." The small flywheel proved to be especially troublesome for him, and his knees would hurt after only an hour of throwing. Adding to these problems was Bresnahan's left handedness, which necessitated kicking the wheel in a counterclockwise direction so he could work with his dominant hand. Bresnahan's frustrations were heightened by Takashi's insistence that he "throw off the hump." With this technique, a large mound of clay is centered on the wheel, and as many as fifty cups or bowls are pulled from the top of the clay before it needs replenishing.

Working this way saves time and thus is economical. More importantly, the mound elevates the object being created to slightly below eye level, allowing the potter to pay close attention to the work's profile. American potters usually hunch over their wheels, thereby concentrating on the interior of their vessels instead of the exteriors.

For practice, Takashi had Bresnahan throw *tōchin* (pillows). Small round forms, *tōchin* serve as kiln furniture, elevating the pieces off the sandy floor of the kiln. In a journal entry from January 25, 1976, Bresnahan noted, "My *tōchin* throwing is getting better. I will have to learn how to throw them perfectly by the end of March because I need to make one thousand of them for the first firing." Soon thereafter, Takashi also showed Bresnahan how to make a basic plate, about five inches in diameter, which he produced in great numbers for gas firings.

But in early February during the midst of building the kiln, Takashi had a falling out with his Japanese apprentices and sent them packing. Bresnahan had sensed rising tensions, but his meager Japanese had not allowed him to understand the situation fully. Shocked and saddened over the loss of his companions, he also grew afraid, thinking he, too, would be told to leave.

Although that did not happen, the incident did radically change Bresnahan's apprenticeship in Japan. As the only one left, he became much more important to Takashi than he normally would have been.

Suddenly, his apprenticeship took on breakneck speed. Out of necessity, Takashi relied on him more and more, and before long, Bresnahan had full responsibility for the daily operations of the studio—a role he would maintain until December 1978 when he returned to the United States.

During that time, Takashi did not establish long-term commitments to any other Japanese apprentices, although young potters did come to the studio for short periods. One exception was Robert Okazaki, a Japanese American from California, who had apprenticed in Bizen for four years with Fujiwara Yu and was engaged to Takashi's niece Keiko. Okazaki arrived at Takashi's studio in the spring of 1976 and shortly thereafter married into the family. He and Bresnahan formed an immediate friendship and soon came to share duties in the studio.

In early March, Bresnahan was taken to dig clay for the first time. In the United States, most pottery studios order clay from manufacturers. But in rural Japan, potters excavate their own clay and in so doing find the blueprint for their personal styles based on its texture, color, and plasticity.

Recognizing that the expedition would be significant for Bresnahan, Takashi made it into a festive excursion. "It was a family event with *sensei*, nephews, nieces, [his] wife, [his daughter] Hanako, and me," Bresnahan recounted in his journal. "We drove the pickup toward the mountain range east of Karatsu. We traveled for about half an hour. After climbing the winding roads, we came to a level area with smaller hills. The red clay was easy to spot—you could see it exposed on the surface of a bank next to a water-soaked rice paddy. It was a hot day, so I dug away with no shirt on. It gave me great satisfaction to know that . . . the bill [would] just [be] the sweat off my brow."

With Keiko's help, construction of the kiln also continued, and by mid-April it was finished. Takashi then called his friend Aoki, a potter from Hachijōjima island, who came with Sumiya, his apprentice. For the next month, Takashi and Aoki devoted themselves to throwing enough ware to fill the large kiln. To keep up with them, Bresnahan wedged six hundred pounds of clay every day, and he and Sumiya worked late into the night, applying slips and glazes to their pots and tea bowls.

On May 4, the loading of the kiln began. Anxious to fire, a dismayed Bresnahan soon discovered how laborious and time-consuming a process it would be. For the first chamber, the potters needed to place small wads of refractory clay under the pieces to prevent them from welding to the kiln floor. For the next three chambers, also without shelves but for glazed ware, they used *tōchin* under the larger vessels and then nestled smaller pots, separated with more wads of refractory clay, inside them. Loading the fifth, or Tanegashima, chamber proved to be most painstaking of all. First, they put shelves between the stoking portals so that wood thrown into the kiln from above would not hit the pottery below. Then, they set some pieces on clay wads; for others, they used rice husks as a refractory material beneath and between them.

They also tossed small clam shells among the pots, hoping their salt content would create interesting color flashing on the vessels nearby. Finally, they loaded the shelves in the salt chamber, placing the wares on more clay wads and liberally strewing crushed shells among them.

To assist with the round-the-clock firing, more people were enlisted, including two of Koyama Fujio's former apprentices. On the evening of May 7, Takashi scattered salt around the kiln to ritually purify it in the ancient Shintō manner and then made offerings of sake, fish, and salt to the gods to ensure a safe and successful result. At 8:30 P.M., he lit the fire, and for the next four days, billowing clouds of steam rose from the chimney as the new kiln cured.

Then on Tuesday morning, May 11, the stoking began in earnest and continued nonstop through Sunday night. Over those six grueling days, the potters, in alternating shifts, fired each chamber in succession, slowly moving toward the back of the kiln and "reading" the flames as they went. Bright orange meant an oxygen-rich atmosphere, relatively lower temperatures, and an active torrent of energy rushing through the chambers; deep, rose-petal red indicated temperatures in excess of 1,000° centigrade, less oxygen, and a slower movement of heat. Dark spots in the orange-red river of fire showed places where the kiln had been loaded too densely, which created cool pockets and would lead to unevenly fired pots in those areas.

After the firing, the kiln took five days to cool before the bricked-up doors could be opened. In the meantime, news reporters, gallery dealers, and art collectors descended on the studio to see the results of Takashi's long-awaited *hatsugama* (first firing). "Everything was being sold," Bresnahan wrote on May 18, 1976. "And I was in a daze at all the people who had come blasting up the hill."

Despite the excitement and buying frenzy, the quality of the pieces was uneven. First firings are notoriously

Honey jar (Takigama kiln, glaze chamber), 1986, stoneware with navy-bean straw ash glaze, 7 in. high. Bresnahan's experiments with navy-bean straw ash began yielding appealing glazes by 1986. If thinly applied, the glaze reacted with the iron in the clay body to produce bluish hues; if thickly applied, it resulted in a milky white color.
Photograph by Gary Mortensen.

unpredictable, and this one was no exception. While the unglazed pieces from the Tanegashima chamber were by far the best and possessed subtle earth tones and velvety textures, the pots from the front chamber lacked the heavy, irregular deposits of ash glaze usually found on works from that section of the kiln. The glazed wares from the next three chambers also were underfired, as were the salt-glazed pieces from the last chamber. To compensate for these deficiencies, Takashi knew that next time they would need to fire the kiln longer and at higher temperatures for better outcomes.

Regardless, the experience became a touchstone for Bresnahan, and the less-than-ideal results led him to carefully analyze the kiln's dynamics, how it was loaded, and the length and intensity of its firing. But despite subsequent adjustments, the kiln continued to be plagued with problems and unable to produce successful wares from all the chambers in a single firing. So after eight more attempts, Takashi decided to construct another kiln more closely based on the *teppogama* he had made on Tanegashima island. In the summer of 1977, he sent Bresnahan there to carefully measure the kiln he had built in 1969.

Teacup (Takigama kiln, glaze chamber), 1981, porcelain with wheat-straw ash glaze, 2 1/2 in. high. Bresnahan always uses local clay and other natural materials at his Saint John's studio. He made the glaze on this early cup from burnt wheat straw, which matured to a surprising range of colors during the firing.
Photograph by Gary Mortensen.

Bresnahan at the wheel shaping a platter with a *hera*, a curved wooden tool traditionally used by Karatsu potters.
Photograph by George Byron Griffiths, 1997.

A few weeks later, he and Bresnahan visited Arita to see how potters there fashioned their own bricks by pounding clay into wooden forms with mallets. Afterward, Bresnahan made thousands of bricks for the new *teppogama* based on their example. He also designed and built the shed roof for the new kiln and, with Takashi's guidance, a system of underground concrete pipes beneath it. In 1969, Takashi and Koyama Fujio had discovered that water sprayed into the kiln during firing created a broad range of colors on unglazed wares, a continuous reduction technique Takashi wanted to utilize in the new *teppogama* as well.

The new kiln was completed and fired in October 1977. Before returning to Minnesota in late 1978, Bresnahan

***Spice jar* (Takigama kiln, glaze chamber), 1982, stoneware with sunflower-seed hull ash glaze, 3 3/4 in. high. Bresnahan advocates using industrial waste materials. He created the golden glaze on this jar by mixing sunflower-seed hull ash (an unwanted by-product at an oil plant) with clay and feldspar.**
Photograph by Gary Mortensen.

participated in three more firings of the *teppogama*. Each firing produced highly admired works with soft textures that were mostly black and gray with dramatic markings of red and orange.

While he had greatly increased his knowledge of kiln construction and firing dynamics, Bresnahan lacked the time to practice throwing after the Japanese apprentices left the studio. By late summer 1976, however, he asked Takashi to resume teaching him on the wheel, and soon, Bresnahan was doggedly spending two hours every evening honing his technique. First, Takashi would demonstrate a particular form and then have Bresnahan duplicate it

precisely. Once a shape had been mastered and could be thrown quickly and in large numbers, Bresnahan was responsible for keeping an inventory of several hundred examples of it for future gas firings.

In general, Bresnahan's training advanced from smaller, simpler forms to larger, more technically demanding ones. Initially, he learned to make small cups for sake (*guinomi*) and tea (*yunomi*). Deeper bowls came later. For *chawan* (bowls for whipped green tea), he also needed to become skilled with the *hera*, a broad, curved wooden tool traditionally used by Karatsu potters. "The high sand content and . . . limited plasticity [of Karatsu clay]," explains

Bresnahan (center) had to expertly produce hundreds of the same form before Nakazato Takashi (back) would teach him a different shape.
March 1978.

Using a Karatsu-style kick wheel, Nakazato Takashi could throw hundreds of bottles during a single sitting, making each one identical in size and shape.
1976.

Sister Johanna Becker, "make it necessary for Karatsu pots to be thrown quickly, with as little added water as possible . . . to avoid collapse of the walls. The *hera* provides an inner support against which the potter can quickly raise the shape while compressing, and thus strengthening, the clay" (Becker, *Karatsu Ware*, p. 152).

Nakazato Takashi, *Vase* (Takashi's Ryūtagama kiln, Tanegashima chamber), 1971, stoneware, 8 in. high.
Photograph by Gary Mortensen.

The ability to produce great numbers of a single vessel in exactly the same shape and size was an integral part of Bresnahan's training. Such accuracy also was a practical necessity. For example, if a teacup were as much as one-sixteenth of an inch too tall, it would not fit into its wooden presentation box. And because the studio preordered huge quantities of such finely crafted boxes, the size of cups was closely prescribed. In other instances, a form's intended use dictated its measurements. Plates for formal meals (*kaiseki*), like those for tea ceremonies, could not be more than 24.3 centimeters in diameter or they would be too big for the wooden trays they were placed on. Finally, some teacups and small plates came in sets

of five. Although some variation between individual objects was permissible and revealed their handmade origins, the pieces still had to seem like a set.

Takashi's high standards and strict discipline ensured that Bresnahan's progress was carefully monitored. Sometimes, it also led the apprentice to despair. "All of the pottery work for the last two months has been in vain," Bresnahan wrote in late April 1977. "The lips of [my] pots have all been too small and straight, so *sensei* made [me] another example. My cutting wires were all bad and my feet were too shallow. So I wedged up new clay, went and got my clothes out of the rain, and cried. Sometimes I want to quit. But it is a turning point. I went back and learned how to make a proper wire and concentrated on the lip form. The small plates I threw came out nicer."

In addition to accuracy, speed was also paramount. Naturally, the studio's financial success depended on the potters' ability to fill orders and meet deadlines. The sandy texture of Karatsu clay also required that pieces be thrown quickly, before too much moisture was drawn out and the clay slumped. But most importantly, speed and precision demonstrated an unconscious mastery of the clay, an intuitive understanding of it that ultimately became apparent in the unity of the object itself. Bresnahan had observed this early in his apprenticeship by watching Takashi work. "He started throwing pitchers," he wrote in his journal. "The rhythm

Bottle with three lugs **(Takigama kiln, front fire chamber), 1984, stoneware with salt glaze, 9 3/4 in. high. Bresnahan based the elongated form of this bottle on ancient Greek amphoras.**
Photograph by Gary Mortensen.

is pure and as the form grows it twists and bends, and I watch like an over-caring parent. It's a volley of perfect harmony with hands and clay. It leaves me breathless to see the fantastic, clean, crisp, soft moist form in such a refined shape." As the apprenticeship progressed, Takashi not only taught Bresnahan how to create new forms but gave him specified time periods to master them. On January 20, 1978, for example, he showed Bresnahan how to throw a rice bowl and then required him to complete five hundred of them in a week. Although Bresnahan met the deadline, the bowls did not meet Takashi's high standards and ended up in the stamper. Bresnahan then had to make five hundred more. By that time, however, Bresnahan took such criticism in stride. Late the same month, he wrote in his journal: "I haven't been anywhere since Christmas. [But] as each day goes on, it feels better and the rhythm sinks deeper . . . . This will be the most intensive study I will ever be able to have—for it will be difficult to work from morning to early [the next] morning on just pottery back home."

By the spring of 1978, Bresnahan's throwing ability had reached an impressive level of competency, and he could finish five hundred *guinomi* (sake cups) in one day. But although he mastered many shapes, Bresnahan saw Takashi throwing many more. He carefully described those forms and how they were created in his journal. These observances also kept the young potter modest, reminding him of how much more he still had to learn. But he also recognized that he could spend a lifetime studying Japan's rich ceramic history and thriving pottery traditions and never be able to know it all.

By late summer 1978, Bresnahan decided it was time to return to the United States. By assisting with the construction of two kilns and expending enormous energy to keep the studio afloat after the departure of the Japanese apprentices, he had served his teacher well. And in a final act of loyalty to him, he agreed to delay his departure until after the fourth firing of the *teppogama* in mid-November. During the busy preparations for the firing, Takashi invited thirty guests to dinner one beautiful fall evening. Like other occasions when important collectors and dignitaries were visiting, an elaborate feast was prepared and sake served. But the guest of honor that night was Bresnahan himself. Dressed in a fine silk kimono and surrounded by all the people who had become his extended family, Bresnahan felt an overwhelming sense of belonging to that exotic faraway place.

Midway through the celebration, local television crews arrived, and Takashi stood to deliver a speech. He praised Bresnahan for his devotion to the studio and his hard work. He complimented him on his tenacity at learning potting techniques and his formidable knowledge of kiln construction and firing methods. In light of all these accomplishments, Takashi concluded, Bresnahan had attained an unusual level of training for any apprentice and one that had earned him the title of "master potter."

Richard Bresnahan thought of that evening and those remarks while he rode the train from Karatsu to Tokyo in early December 1978. But as he boarded the plane for the flight home, he also remembered what Sister Johanna had said to him before leaving Minnesota: "You will never be Japanese, Richard. Don't forget who you are."

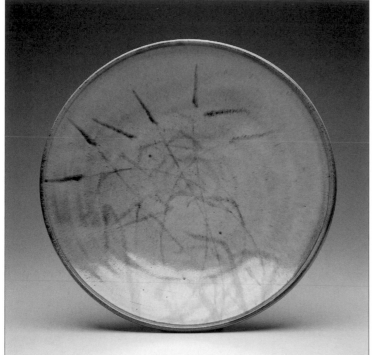

Platter (Johanna kiln, glaze chamber), 1998, stoneware with iron painting over a navy-bean straw ash glaze, 16 5/16 in. diameter.
Photograph by Gary Mortensen.

The Pottery at Saint John's University

Walking with crutches, Richard Bresnahan was released from the hospital in North Dakota on June 8, 1979. While convalescing, he had decided to accept President Michael Blecker's invitation to set up a pottery in Minnesota at Saint John's University. But Bresnahan was equally determined to operate the studio in a fundamentally different way than most university-sponsored programs. His studio would be run by three to four potters whose financial existence would largely depend on their own self-sufficiency. They would construct a kiln without incurring significant debt, find and treat locally available materials, and derive a living through the sale of their pottery. In this way, Bresnahan reasoned, he could use his experience in Japan and give aspiring potters a way to support themselves monetarily while remaining true to their passion for ceramics.

Sauce containers **(Johanna kiln, front fire chamber), 1999, stoneware with natural ash glaze, 6¹⁄₁₆ in. high (left and center), 6¹⁄₄ in. high (right). Bresnahan often devises new forms to meet his own needs. In 1999, he created these small containers to hold soy sauce and olive oil. Adding whimsy to their already zoomorphic shapes, he outfitted each spout with a gilded champagne cork.**
Photograph by Gary Mortensen.

To adhere to his own personal convictions, he also would manage the studio in an environmentally responsible way by using recycled goods or waste materials whenever possible. Rather than placing orders with companies whose mining and manufacturing practices contributed to ecological degradation, he would locate native plants that could be processed on site for glazes. Clay would be prepared at the studio as well. And he would build a Korean-style *noborigama* to derive maximum fuel usage by routing the heat through several chambers filled with pots before it escaped out the chimney.

Of course, Bresnahan also had aesthetic reasons for wanting to construct a *noborigama*. While in Japan, he had come to like the dynamic, mostly uncontrolled effects possible from firing with wood. Unlike a gas kiln's predictable results, wood firings create pottery marked by serendipity and the potent atmosphere of the kiln interior. Dramatic color variations also result from the movement of the fiery torrent as it rushes through the structure, enveloping the pots. In the fire storm of the first chamber, especially, wood ash settles on the tops and fronts of the vessels, then liquefies and runs in glassy rivulets across the clay surfaces. While gravity pulls the molten glass downward, the force of the fire can also push it horizontally as it travels back through the kiln. Such striking effects elevate a wood firing into a unique collaboration between potter and nature.

Bottle **(Johanna kiln, front fire chamber), 2000, stoneware with iron slip painting and natural ash glaze, 9 in. high. The greatest color variations and textures appear on wares placed in the first chamber of the Johanna kiln, where the directional thrust of the fire is strongest and carries with it large amounts of ash and other particles from the burning wood. This simple bottle shows the accidental—but dramatic—effects that occur in the stormy atmosphere of the front fire chamber.**
Photograph by Gary Mortensen.

Additionally, Bresnahan wanted to make the studio an integral part of a larger community—not only with the university and monastery but also with the neighboring towns of Collegeville, St. Joseph, Avon, and St. Cloud. While a student at Saint John's, he had come to admire the frugality and diligence of the Benedictine brothers, some of whom even made furniture for the campus dormitories and classrooms. He discovered they rarely threw anything away and carefully salvaged doors, windows, paneling, fixtures, and other hardware when structures were razed or remodeled. In the hands of Benedictine carpenters, such discards were given new life. Bresnahan also was awed to learn the monks themselves had molded and fired hundreds of thousands of red bricks for the original church and surrounding buildings. And he hoped the studio, too, would become part of this living tradition that equated the creation of useful objects, however humble, with worship.

In a like manner, Bresnahan also revered farmers and their families, whose love of the land and backbreaking labor brought food to the table. He understood the difficulties of rural life and the necessity of hard work coupled with ingenuity. Perhaps in a somewhat romantic way, he liked to think the pottery could also serve a purpose in a farm community by producing functional objects for daily use. He certainly felt a greater familiarity and sense of belonging with farmers than with gallery owners and art collectors. To be true to his own identity, he wanted the locals to find the studio a welcoming and useful place as well. He was equally resolute in his desire to make pottery that was unique to central Minnesota, a goal that could be attained by capitalizing on locally available materials. In Japan, pottery from each region is readily identifiable. Pots from Shigaraki, for example, have textural surfaces dotted with white feldspar, which occurs naturally in

In 1979, Bresnahan converted the basement of St. Joseph Hall at Saint John's University into a pottery studio. He used the adjoining garage for clay storage and processing.
Photograph by Mark Strand, 1980.

50

clay from that area. In contrast, clay from Bizen is fine and smooth with a high iron content that results in rich brown hues when fired. If Bresnahan could find a local deposit of clay that was suitable for potting, he could create a Saint John's "look" based on its particular color and composition.

Bresnahan arrived at Saint John's University on June 18, 1979, ready to actualize his dreams but somewhat daunted by what lay ahead. "Now begins the mammoth task of getting clay and starting to set up a pottery," he wrote at the time. "There is so much work it is unbelievable."

Saint John's had decided to allocate space for the new studio in the basement of St. Joseph Hall and its adjoining garage. "Joe" Hall had been built by the monks in 1923. Its first floor had originally been a livery and its upper floors housing for lay workers who were employed by the university. Later, it was converted into a student dormitory. For Bresnahan, the 3,200-square-foot basement, formerly a root cellar for cheese storage, and the 1,800-square-foot heated garage provided plenty of room for his new enterprise. The basement's cavernous corbel-vaulted spaces also offered an added bonus: they were ideal as damp rooms—humid areas where pottery could be dried slowly without cracking.

Bresnahan hired David Landwehr, a local wood-worker, to build three Karatsu-style kick wheels from waste mahogany he had purchased inexpensively from a local valve manufacturer. Bresnahan also salvaged an old Hobart industrial kitchen mixer for processing clay and stretched army-surplus nylon

(from parachutes) between two rusted I-beams for drying it. He even constructed racks for drying pottery from discarded lengths of plumbing pipe.

At the same time, Bresnahan began to look for local clay deposits. He learned of a relatively pure vein at a defunct brick factory in Paynesville, Minnesota, but its depth made excavation impossible. He talked with county extension agents and checked land surveys at the local library but found nothing. He even called well-drilling companies to ask if they had ever hit a clay deposit while drilling. Only one had and the kaolin they discovered in Richmond, Minnesota, was ninety feet below the surface and owned by the Tennessee Ball Clay Company.

Bresnahan explained his dilemma to anyone who would listen, and at last, a friend suggested he visit Rosemary Petters, a potter who had been given a bucket of clay by a local man several months before. In fact, Petters still had the black clay and gladly turned it over to Bresnahan. By processing it, he determined it to be very pure, without the usual contaminates found in soils once covered by glacial ice. It was finely grained and plastic, similar to Bizen clay, and not at all like Karatsu clay with its impurities and sandy composition. Bresnahan called Petters with a barrage of questions: Where could this clay possibly have come from? Who had brought it to her? Could he meet him?

She put him in contact with a remarkable person—Francis Schellinger. Trained as a professional carpenter, Schellinger had retired in his early fifties and during the 1970s had become a forerunner of the "back to earth" movement when he purchased 180 acres of deciduous forest in Collegeville, Minnesota. There, he built a house, raised a family, and lived simply, spending his time learning about and exploring the world around him. He milled his own lumber, grew his own food, made maple syrup, and kept honeybees. He knew everyone and befriended many, especially young artists who were trying to eke out a living while renovating old farmhouses in the area. He had even built a small cabin on his property to temporarily house individuals in need. To this day, he is renowned locally for his exceptional wisdom, gentle soul, and quick wit. In fact, he recently declared, on seeing Bresnahan driving a 1979 Dodge van covered with rust, that he had finally found someone even more frugal than he.

As soon as Schellinger heard Bresnahan's story, he escorted him to an abandoned stretch of road on nearby Lake Watab. Bulldozers had ripped through the topsoil there, uncovering a seam of clay thirty-five-feet wide and forty-feet deep. Schellinger had come across the clay one day when he was out looking for agates with his children, and he had returned home with a few bucketfuls. "But how did you know it was clay?" Bresnahan asked. Schellinger responded very matter-of-factly: "I tasted it." "You tasted it?" Bresnahan repeated in disbelief. "Richard," Schellinger said, "Haven't you ever heard of the Georgia clay eaters?"

An excited Bresnahan returned to Saint John's and asked for permission to have the clay relocated to the campus. Father James Tingerthal and Brother Mark Kelly, who were in charge of the monastery's grounds, set aside an area behind Saint John's Preparatory School and its baseball field. Then, Schellinger spoke to the planning committee of Collegeville township on Bresnahan's behalf, explaining that the clay caused drainage problems and urging them to allow the potter to excavate it provided he pay for replacement fill. The committee agreed and soon 175 truckloads of the black material—some 18,000 tons of it—were dumped at Saint John's over a five-day period. The resulting hillock caused great consternation among many of the resident monks, who wondered aloud what they might expect next from the young upstart. But Bresnahan felt euphoric, and although he had suddenly gone $3,600 in debt, he had about $500,000 worth of clay stockpiled—more than enough to last his lifetime and a few more.

That July 4 to celebrate his 26th birthday, Bresnahan threw seven large bowls from the new clay. It was the first time he had worked on the wheel since returning from Japan six months earlier. As the spinning mound of clay took shape under his hands, the daunting task of setting up the pottery somehow seemed less insurmountable. And the difficulties of the last several months—the disruption of returning home after a long absence, the ever-present concern about money, and the accident—seemed to fade away. Sitting at the wheel, he felt sure of himself again, of his abilities, and the decisions he had made while hospitalized.

Next, Bresnahan turned his attention to constructing a kiln. To solidify his presence on campus, he strongly felt he should stage the first firing that very fall. Adding to the urgency was the need to complete the structure before temperatures dropped below freezing—a circumstance that could occur in Minnesota by early autumn.

Shortly after his arrival at Saint John's, Bresnahan had met Laurie Hallberg, who taught ceramics at nearby St. Cloud State University. Hallberg had once purchased seventy-five tons of used brick from Northern States Power Company with the intention of building his own kiln. But he agreed to sell Bresnahan what he needed at a discount if Bresnahan and his cadre of volunteers would help him clean and sort all of his stock. In the end, Bresnahan not only used Hallberg's bricks but cast-off brick from a demolished incinerator at Saint John's

to line the kiln and discarded floor tile from another building on campus to buttress the kiln walls. The kiln's cast arch was comprised of aluminate cement mixed with ten tons of broken firebrick, which Bresnahan had convinced a local gravel company to run through its rock crusher for a mere seventy-five dollars. Ultimately, the kiln cost $1,500 to build—a savings of more than $50,000 had new materials been purchased.

Still wearing a full-leg cast, Bresnahan had little hope of actually building the kiln himself. He appealed to Abbot Jerome Theisen for help, who assigned five novices to work at the studio as part of their daily afternoon labor. Thanos Johnson, who had visited Bresnahan twice in Japan and was a potter at the College of Marin in

Double-gourd teapot **(Johanna kiln, front fire chamber), 1995, stoneware with iron slip and natural ash glaze, 8 in. high. Reed handle by Paul Krueger. Starting in 1986, Bresnahan began using an iron-rich clay slip on some of his pots to create deep brown, black, and purple hues, which he associated with the black Seto ware so admired by Japanese tea enthusiasts.**
Photograph by Gary Mortensen.

Kentfield, California, also sent two of his students, Alan Peirson and Douglas Smith, who became Bresnahan's first apprentices. And even Bresnahan's 12-year-old brother, Chad, helped by laying the floor of the fire-mouth chamber, a space far too small for Bresnahan to negotiate with his broken leg.

Bresnahan designed his kiln, with some modifications, after the first wood-burning kiln he had helped Takashi build in Japan. Bresnahan's *noborigama* consisted of five chambers: a front fire-mouth, three glaze chambers, and a final chamber for unglazed wares. He created space for it in a long, low machine shed adjoining the garage, which alleviated the need to erect a separate shed roof. Construction began in late July and, miraculously, was finished two months later. Abbot Jerome blessed the kiln, which Bresnahan had named Takigama, after Takashi's son Taki. Working nearly around the clock, Bresnahan and his two new apprentices also made enough pots to fill the kiln for its first firing—which began on November 22, 1979, nearly a year after the potter's return to Minnesota.

While the results were somewhat erratic—some of the glazed pieces were unevenly fired, and many of the pots had surface blistering from the clay being insufficiently processed—the new kiln held great promise. Objects from the last chamber, especially, displayed a wide range of subtle earth tones, from cool grays and blues to deep burgundies, fiery reds, and pale oranges.

Bresnahan's experiments with locally derived glazes had yielded encouraging results as well. Ash from flax straw, gathered at his uncle Leo's farm in central North Dakota and mixed with feldspar and local clay, had produced a milky hue that blushed blue. From the Sinner-Bresnahan farm in Casselton, North Dakota, came a wheat-straw ash that rendered a whitish tint, which sometimes ran to a transparent pale green, and a navy-bean ash that created a vibrant blue. Even elm ash from Francis Schellinger's wood-burning stove had made a semitransparent glaze with bluish-lavender highlights. Only the coal ash Bresnahan had collected from Saint John's own power plant had resulted in a less than desirable color—a muddy gray.

Bresnahan's first kiln at Saint John's was a five-chamber *noborigama*, which he named Takigama after his Japanese master's son.
Photograph by James R. Dean, May 1992.

Bresnahan (center) with his apprentice Samuel Johnson burning flax straw at the family farm in North Dakota. Mixed with feldspar and clay, the flax-straw ash produces a milky bluish glaze.
Photograph by Todd Hunter Strand, October 1996.

Most importantly, however, the drama of the first firing had captivated the entire monastery and university. Centrally located, the kiln had sent clouds of steam and smoke drifting through the campus when the firing began. At the height of stoking, flames shot dramatically upward from the chimney. Like a beacon, they enticed the curious from miles around, including the monastery's own brigade of firefighters. Successive firings proved to be equally sensational and well attended. Volunteers, including students from the university and residents from the surrounding townships— would camp on the lawn around the studio in what quickly became a community happening. And during football season, throngs of spectators would hurry over to the kiln after the games, and, in between stoking, Bresnahan would often serve them exotic green teas.

But while the pottery was up and running in record time, its future was far from secure. It was independent of the art department and other established programs on campus, and some monks thought it did not belong at Saint John's at all. But after the success of the first firing, Abbot Jerome Theisen and President Michael Blecker gave Bresnahan what Blecker called a "fingernail hold on the university" by establishing a permanent position for him, teaching a month-long class each year in January. Bresnahan offered his first course in 1980 and focused on two of his passions—Japan and environmentalism. In a determined move to safeguard the pottery's existence on campus, he returned his wages to Saint John's as rent for the studio's space. For those who criticized Blecker's decision to appoint Bresnahan as artist-in-residence because it made little financial sense, the gesture appeared conciliatory. For everyone else, it seemed an act of astounding self-sacrifice.

Modest but meaningful support from outside the university also began to arrive shortly after the studio opened. In late 1979, Bresnahan received a Bush Foundation grant, and in 1980, he, along with the studio, was awarded funding from the National Endowment for the Arts. By fall 1981, the Grotto Foundation provided money for the pottery's apprentices, and beginning in 1983, the Jerome Foundation supplied grants for visiting artists.

Between 1979 and 1991, Bresnahan fired the Takigama kiln two to three times annually. In addition to viewing the spectacular firings, people came to the studio's sales and, in the early years, could purchase small pots for two or three dollars apiece. While the income did little to subsidize the studio, the sales helped establish a regular clientele for the pottery and make it known to a wider public.

At the same time, John Pellegrene, a senior vice president of marketing at the Dayton Hudson Corporation, became aware of Bresnahan's work in 1981 when he saw posters advertising a solo exhibition of his at the Plains Art Museum. After visiting the studio, Pellegrene invited Bresnahan to be the featured artist at the downtown Minneapolis store's spring flower show in 1984. During the event, Bresnahan gave throwing demonstrations and exhibited his work, all the while explaining his nature-based, environmentally responsible approach to pottery making. With thousands of visitors daily, the company's aggressive advertising campaign, and local newspaper coverage, Bresnahan and the pottery gained considerable notoriety. Bresnahan's pots also were featured at five other Dayton Hudson department

stores and sold through the company's catalogue. Besides being a lucrative experience for the potter, the prestigious association with one of the region's greatest retailers helped to validate his work, both philosophically and artistically.

A similar relationship also developed between Bresnahan and the Spiegel Catalogue Company, which wanted to profile the potter in spring 1991 as a way of showing their support for Earth Day. In fact, Saint John's alumnus James Clark, who worked for a marketing firm handling some of Spiegel's promotions in Chicago, brokered the deal. The company's buyers chose a teapot and a vase for their catalogue, and suddenly, information on Bresnahan, his art, and his environmental commitment found its way into forty million households across America. Still, it was a dubious sort of fame, Bresnahan knew, one that depended less on his integrity as an artist than on Spiegel's ability to turn a popular interest in ecology into a sellable product. As with Dayton Hudson, however, when Spiegel suggested mass producing Bresnahan's designs to reduce costs and sell larger quantities, the potter respectfully declined.

During the fall of 1992, Bresnahan conducted the last firing of the Takigama kiln. Saint John's planned to erect a new student center on the site of Joe Hall and told Bresnahan he needed to vacate the building by May 1993. Far from signaling an end to the studio, however, this decision heralded its rebirth. As a testament to how much Bresnahan and the pottery had become a valued part of the Saint John's community, the monks not only voted to continue the

Bottles (Johanna kiln, glaze chamber), 2000, stoneware with porcelain and iron slip painting under a flax-straw ash glaze and an elm ash glaze, 7 1/2 in. high (left), 7 in. high (right). Depending on their placement in the glaze chamber, pots will often display radically different surface effects. Here, the bottle on the left was near the front of the chamber, where ash sometimes enters from the front of the kiln. As the ash settled on the vessel, it liquified and combined with the glaze to create a subtle "hare's fur." The vessel on the right was positioned farther back in the chamber and thus remained "unblemished."

Photograph by Gary Mortensen.

Bresnahan (right) in the Saint John's Pottery with his apprentice Samuel Johnson.

Photograph by James R. Dean, May 1997.

program but to move Joe Hall to a different location on campus. Its reconstruction would include space for a new pottery, and a new kiln would be built a short distance away near Stumpf Lake.

Bresnahan seized this opportunity to design an even more efficient studio space. Construction of a new foundation for Joe Hall meant that some drawbacks of the old studio could be corrected. The new space, for instance, would all be on the same level, enabling large pieces to be moved around on wheeled platforms instead of by hand. When the concrete floor was poured, multiple drains were included, allowing the studio to be easily and frequently washed down—a procedure that reduces dust, a health hazard for potters. To underscore the studio's commitment to ecology, Bresnahan also incorporated a water treatment system, so that water used in processing raw clay can be recycled, and energy-efficient fluorescent lights. In addition, Bresnahan asked sculptor Sugi Kazuaki to design and construct a gas kiln to replace the old electric one. Well insulated with soft refractory brick and equipped with twenty-six burners, the new gas kiln operates at maximum energy efficiency. Its wheeled platform and sliding door also make for easy loading of large-scale pots and sculpture.

Even before the Takigama kiln was dismantled, Bresnahan began designing a new structure that scarcely resembles its predecessor at all. Most remarkable is its scale—at a length of eighty-seven feet with an interior capacity of 1,600 cubic feet, it is the largest wood-burning kiln in North America. The new structure has three chambers, instead of

the Takigama's five: a front fire-mouth, a glaze chamber, and a Tanegashima chamber. Several factors prompted Bresnahan to build on such a grand scale. When he studied in Japan, he visited old kiln sites with Koyama Shin'ichi, who explained how the country's enormous old kilns could hold the wares of many potters, thus making firings communal affairs, and that their vast interior spaces directly led to the surface effects so admired on ancient vessels. Modern potters had little chance of duplicating those effects, Koyama said, given the relatively small size of their kilns. Thus, to serve the needs of a variety of artists and to create the kind of internal environment necessary to achieve his own aesthetic goals, Bresnahan planned his kiln accordingly. To accommodate large-scale sculpture, he once again enlisted the help of Sugi Kazuaki, who welded huge steel doors for the front and back of the kiln. Suspended from wheels that run along an overhead I-beam, the doors can be pushed aside during loading and unloading. The kiln's scale also allows for more pottery to be fired at once, thus making maximum use of fuel expenditure. The kiln's large interior also means there are fewer firings—only one a year—and that more is at stake on each occasion.

In addition to its unusual size, Bresnahan's kiln included several innovations. Recalling ancient *anagama* in Tokoname that have central pillars inside the kiln to divide the flame, Bresnahan outfitted his front chamber with twin stoking boxes, which he located at the front corners of the chamber. By moving the kiln shelves to the center of the space, away from the back and side walls, he enabled the flames to travel up the side walls and across the arched ceiling

Left to right: Sugi Kazuaki, Joe McLaughlin, James LaChance, Tom Mars, and Bresnahan near the partially built Tanegashima chamber of the Johanna kiln. Thirty volunteers worked for two years to complete the kiln.
Photograph by James R. Dean, August 1993.

Bresnahan now operates a three-chamber *noborigama* at Saint John's University, which he named after his mentor, Sister Johanna Becker. Completed in October 1994, the 87-foot-long Johanna kiln has an interior capacity of 1,600 cubic feet.
Photograph by Greg Becker, 1995.

Five-footed melon-shaped plate (Johanna kiln, Tanegashima chamber), 1998, stoneware, 10 1/2 in. diameter.
Bresnahan created the large circular marking on this plate by inverting it onto a wide-mouthed bowl and then firing it in that position. By packing wild rice hulls and seashells in the space between the plate and the bowl, he achieved the subtle luster and undulating "skin" of the plate's dark center.
Photograph by Gary Mortensen.

in a dynamic double-helix pattern. As a result, fly ash is lifted and distributed throughout the chamber, forming glazes even on the back-facing sides of pieces. Secondly, he not only pierced the front and back walls of the second chamber with flues at ground level, which is typical, but at the top as well. In so doing, he achieved an even heat distribution throughout the first and second chambers.

Sister Johanna Becker and Bresnahan near the dedicatory plaque for the Johanna kiln with photographer Greg Becker.
Photograph by James R. Dean, October 1994.

But perhaps the most radical innovation he devised is at the back of the kiln—a subterranean flue that leads to the chimney and has seven small portal dampers. Positioned lower than the third chamber, this long narrow tunnel forces the heat and flame downward and through its thirty-seven-foot length. The resulting back pressure slows the fire's journey throughout the entire kiln, and the flue's dampers enable the kiln's internal atmosphere to be adjusted, compensating for even slight fluctuations in barometric pressure.

Finally, drawing inspiration from Koyama Fujio and Takashi's experiments with water, Bresnahan designed a series of channels underneath the third chamber of his new kiln. By pouring small amounts of water into these channels each morning as the barometric pressure begins to rise, he can clear out the carbon from the previous night's stoking and create a variety of atmospheric conditions in the Tanegashima chamber, which result in a wide range of colors on his unglazed pots.

Like the Takigama kiln, the new kiln was largely built from recycled materials. Bricks from the original root cellar of Joe Hall and the Takigama kiln were carefully cleaned and reused. Bresnahan also visited Northern States Power Company in Becker, Minnesota, which was relining its Sherco 3 plant's enormous chimney with new brick. Given the height of the stack, imperfect or damaged bricks are routinely replaced to avoid structural weaknesses. The company's managers gladly let Bresnahan have their discarded bricks, which also saved them the expense of disposal.

The massive new kiln took two years to build and the efforts of thirty volunteers. Finally, in a ceremony officiated by Abbot Timothy Kelly and University President Dietrich Reinhart, the kiln was blessed on October 12, 1994. To honor Sister Johanna Becker's pivotal role in his education and her enduring friendship, Bresnahan named the kiln after her. And it was she who had the privilege of lighting it on October 13, 1995, for its first firing.

The Johanna kiln yielded spectacular results from the very beginning. Works from the front chamber, where the temperature is hottest, bore heavy deposits of natural ash glazing in shimmering blues, greens, and ambers. Objects from the second chamber had applied glazes made from sunflower hull ash, navy-bean hull ash, flax ash with *temmoku*, and oak, elm, and basswood ash, whereas unglazed wares from the third chamber featured dramatic color variations, from smoky grays and blues to vivid reds, oranges, and ochers. And amazingly, after ten days of continuous stoking, very little breakage occurred, and more than ninety-five percent of the 8,000 pieces in the kiln emerged intact. The pots from the first firing were so visually compelling that The Minneapolis Institute of Arts featured seventy of them in a special exhibition at the museum the following year.

Since its initial firing, the Johanna kiln has been lit four more times, usually in mid-October before Minnesota's falling temperatures make it too difficult to unload and wash the objects afterward. Adjustments in placement, fluctuations in weather, and the scale of the works themselves have made each firing different. Pots from the second firing and the front fire chamber, for example, had the heaviest deposits of natural ash glaze Bresnahan has ever seen, with the shoulders and bodies of large jars nearly encased in glassy rivulets. In contrast, the most stunning color variations on pieces from the third, or Tanegashima, chamber occurred during the fourth and fifth firings. And for each firing, Bresnahan adopts a few new forms while dropping others from his repertoire.

Stoking the Tanegashima chamber of the Johanna kiln during its first firing.
Photograph by James R. Dean, October 1995.

Serving bowl (Nakazato Takashi's Ryūtagama kiln, front fire chamber), 1976, stoneware with natural ash glaze, 7 1/4 in. high. This large bowl reflects the American preference for communal dining. Made during Bresnahan's apprenticeship in Japan, it possesses an unusually even coating of natural ash glaze from the first chamber of Takashi's kiln. Photograph by Gary Mortensen.

The Works

Bresnahan does not consider the prodigious number of works he created during his student years to be part of his artistic output. The pottery he initially made at Saint John's—from preprocessed clays, shaped on electric wheels, and fired in gas or electric kilns—had little to do with the direction he would ultimately take. Likewise, the vast majority of pieces he produced as Takashi's apprentice are virtually indistinguishable from those of his teacher.

A few works from Bresnahan's time in Japan, however, do represent his own uniqueness. In 1976, he threw a large serving bowl for the first firing of Takashi's *noborigama*. The bowl not only reveals Bresnahan's struggle to master the

Vase (Nakazato Takashi's Ryūtagama kiln, Tanegashima chamber), 1976, stoneware, 8 in. high. Fired in the first kiln Bresnahan helped build in Karatsu for his Japanese teacher, this vase derives its overall shape from the Pueblo Indian ollas of the American Southwest. For the decoration, Bresnahan incised the shoulder with the combed wave patterns commonly found on prehistoric Korean and Japanese pottery.
Photograph by Gary Mortensen.

sandy Karatsu clay, a task made all the more difficult by the vessel's generous scale, but the American preference for communal dining. To an extent, the bowl also shows the influence of American potter Peter Voulkos, who once enlarged a Japanese tea bowl to a fantastic size for dramatic effect. While Bresnahan's work still functions as a bowl, its shape mimics a traditional tea bowl with a notched foot.

Another piece Bresnahan made for the 1976 firing was a vase with a wide mouth, a broad shoulder, and a rounded bottom. Bresnahan associated the form with the Pueblo Indian ollas from the American Southwest. His design, however, includes a combed wave pattern on the shoulder, a technique commonly seen on prehistoric pottery from Korea and Japan.

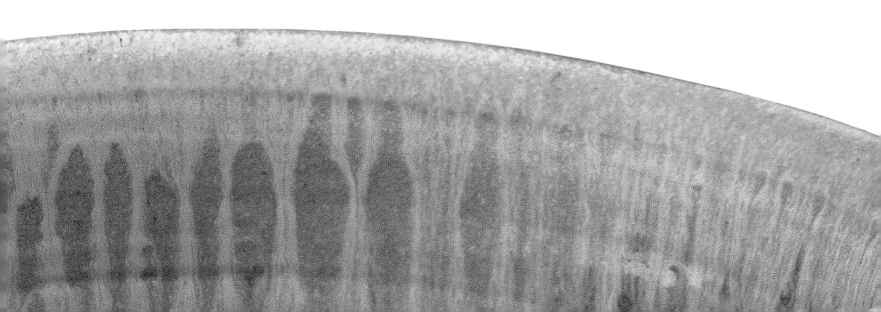

Plate (Nakazato Takashi's Ryūtagama kiln, glaze chamber), 1978, stoneware with inlaid Korean porcelain under a transparent glaze, 9 in. diameter. While in Japan, Bresnahan produced countless *mishima* dishes and bowls decorated with carved and stamped inlaid designs. Here, he playfully substituted an American motif—galloping horses—for the floral patterns normally found on such wares.
Photograph by Gary Mortensen.

Landscape platter (Johanna kiln, Tanegashima chamber), 1998, stoneware with white slip painting, 14 in. diameter.
Photograph by Gary Mortensen.

Landscape plate (Takigama kiln, glaze chamber), 1979, stoneware with white slip painting and inlay under an elm ash glaze, 11 1/2 in. diameter. After returning from Japan, Bresnahan sought inspiration in the rural Midwestern landscape.
Photograph by Gary Mortensen.

Geometric landscape platter
(Johanna kiln, Tanegashima
chamber), 1995, stoneware with iron
painting and slip trailing, 14 1/4 in.
diameter. Bresnahan's landscape
platters show aerial views of fenced,
plowed, and irrigated farmland. For
him, the geometric patterns also
allude to humankind's relentless
subjugation of nature.
Photograph by Gary Mortensen.

One of the first tasks Bresnahan had at Takashi's studio was to apply white slip to the *mishima* ware. After quickly brushing the surface of the pot with slip, he would then scrape away the excess to reveal the incised or stamped patterns underneath. For a plate he made for himself in October 1978, Bresnahan playfully substituted an American motif—galloping horses—for the floral designs normally found on such pieces.

While unable to develop this idea further in Japan, he did create a number of inlaid designs after his return to the Midwest. Among the earliest of these were platters featuring the plowed fields of rural Minnesota and North Dakota. Cutting into the platter's surface, he rendered the fields with rows of precise straight lines, which he then carefully filled with slip. In contrast, he represented the sky—with its billowy cumulus clouds—freely, using a brush loaded with slip. Eventually, he simplified his approach by quickly applying a swath of white slip to the lower half of the plate and then carving in the fields with his thumbnail while the slip was still moist.

Over time, Bresnahan developed two variations on this theme. On platters, he painted and slip-trailed geometric patterns to depict aerial views of fenced, plowed, and irrigated land. On the exterior surfaces of bowls, he deeply incised parallel V-shaped troughs to suggest plowed furrows. He left the earliest of these, from the mid-1980s, unglazed, allowing the iron-rich clay of the bowl itself to resemble freshly turned earth. Later, he applied navy-bean ash glazes to the pots, creating dramatic contrasts between the milky glaze, which runs into the cuts, and the dark clay body, which becomes prominent where the glaze pulls away from the sharp ridges. He also carved similar images into tall, narrow pitchers and brushed them with iron oxides, which result in warm burnt oranges, before applying his navy-bean glazes.

Although Bresnahan enjoyed the freedom of slip painting, he continued to produce inlaid designs. He based some of these on models he learned from Takashi, like the twenty tea bowls he made in 1987

Covered bowl **(Johanna kiln, glaze chamber), 1999, stoneware with navy-bean straw ash glaze, 8 1/8 in. high (with lid). Bresnahan draws inspiration from the plowed fields of rural Minnesota and North Dakota. He softened the sharp ridges of the carved furrows on this bowl by coating it with a thick layer of glaze.**
Photograph by Gary Mortensen.

Spouted bowl (Takigama kiln, Tanegashima chamber), 1986, stoneware with inlaid white slip and iron painting, 17 ¼ in. wide. Bresnahan made this dynamically shaped bowl to celebrate the birth of his first child.
Photograph by Gary Mortensen.

on commission. For these, he utilized a rope-and-floral inlay in the *mishima* style and then incised the inside bottom of each bowl with a Latin cross. In 1985, to celebrate the birth of his first child, he created a series of platters and large horseshoe-shaped bowls titled *Breast-Feeding Angels*. Using slip inlays in a much more dynamic manner, he carved powerful nude women with wings tenderly caressing their babies. A few years later, to honor his longtime friend and supporter Father Michael Blecker who died after a protracted illness, Bresnahan did a similar series, only this time the child on the jars symbolizes Blecker's soul, being passed heaven-ward from angel to angel.

Between 1980 and 1983, Bresnahan also made a series of large cylindrical shapes with inlaid images of fish. He drew inspiration for these sculptural forms from the bollards, or wooden posts for mooring lines, he had seen along Lake Superior's North Shore. The color variations and kiln incrustations that occurred naturally during his wood firings also influenced him. Such soft shimmering hues, he believed, helped contribute to the impression of light filtering through water, and the embedded fly ash resembled calcium deposits and barnacles clinging to the posts.

Immediately after returning from Japan, Bresnahan also began making his own *e*-Karatsu ware, using iron oxides to decorate his pots and applying glazes over them. He had desperately wanted to learn how to paint traditional Japanese *e*-Karatsu, which features simplified plants and birds, while he was at Takashi's. But the Japanese never let him because they thought his left-handed brushwork would be too clumsy. Consequently, he sometimes returned to the studio after everyone else had left and secretly practiced, copying the designs Takashi's niece Keiko had painted earlier in the day. Later, before going to bed himself, he would destroy the evidence of these clandestine sessions by running his pieces through the stamper.

Back in the Midwest, however, he started combining *e*-Karatsu painting techniques with images from his own immediate surroundings. Rather than picturing thick sheaves of wheat, for example, which would have been a typical American symbol for abundance, he produced more intimate glimpses of nature, showing only a few stalks of the plant at different

Bollard with fish (Takigama kiln, Tanegashima chamber), 1984, stoneware with white slip inlays, 29 in. high. Bresnahan has always drawn inspiration from his natural surroundings. He based this sculptural form on the bollards, or wooden posts, he saw along Lake Superior's waterfront.
Photograph by Gary Mortensen.

Bowl (Johanna kiln, glaze chamber), 1995, stoneware with navy-bean straw ash glaze over iron oxide painting, 14 in. diameter. Influenced by *e*-Karatsu ware featuring quickly painted birds and plants, Bresnahan began decorating some of his pots in a similar fashion after returning to the Midwest. For this bowl, he rendered Karatsu-style birds with upturned wings. The dense arrangement of parallel lines, however, recalls his boyhood experiences in North Dakota. Wandering through its marshlands, he would sometimes come across thousands of waterfowl, which would startle by his approach and suddenly take flight, darkening the sky overhead.
Photograph by Gary Mortensen.

stages of growth or decline. While wandering through the forests surrounding Saint John's, he also discovered wild grapes and lady slippers, which eventually became motifs on his vessels as well. For the first firing of the Johanna kiln, he even painted dense flocks of birds on some of his large bowls. Using parallel lines to suggest the birds' flight pattern, he drew on his boyhood experiences of the North Dakota countryside, when thousands of waterfowl would suddenly take to the sky, startled by his presence.

Occasionally, Bresnahan's reaction to the world around him had a less idyllic tone. Soon after returning from Japan, for instance, he learned the United States Department of Defense was aggressively recruiting students to join its new all-volunteer army. Having grown up during the Vietnam era, Bresnahan remained highly distrustful of American military policies. In reaction to the government's latest strategies, he designed the *ROTC Cookie Jar* series.

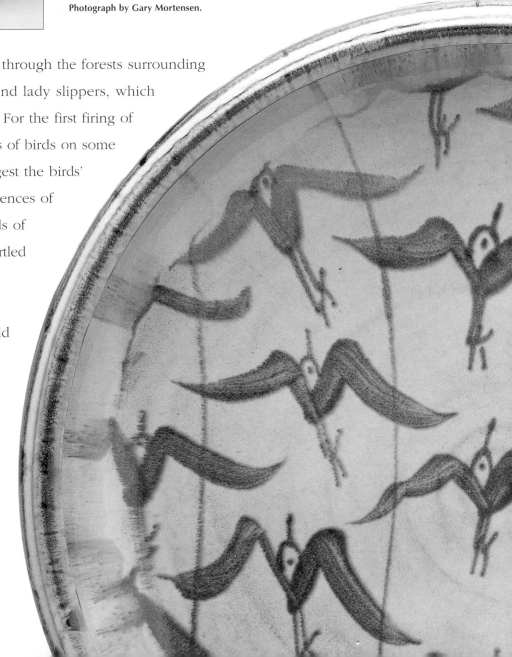

"Paratrooper," from *ROTC Cookie Jar series* (Takigama kiln, Tanegashima chamber), 1980, stoneware, 9 3/4 in. high. Bresnahan, who came of age during the Vietnam era, designed a series of anthropomorphic cookie jars in 1980 that poked fun at the U.S. military. This one, called "Paratrooper," features a potbellied form with clay medals shaped like open parachutes.
Photograph by Gary Mortensen.

During the Depression when sugar was in short supply, a prominently displayed cookie jar containing treats made from the rare commodity proclaimed a family's resourcefulness. Likewise, thrifty housewives used cookie jars as places to store money. So for Bresnahan, the cookie jar not only became a metaphor for the American family and its resilience but for its hopes and dreams. As a way to symbolize the military's intrusion into family life, Bresnahan gave his jars anthropomorphic features. He fashioned his "General" cookie jars with broad "shoulders" and expansive "chests" decorated with clay commendation medals.

The "Aerospace Division" jars are tall and tapered at the neck like bomb casings, and the "POW" jars feature emaciated bodies with torn handles, broken medals, and barbed-wire scratches. And for "Paratrooper," in the "Retired Macho" series, he created a potbellied form with downturned handles to suggest weak, flabby arms and a "chest" cluttered with medals shaped like open parachutes.

At the same time he was developing his repertoire of forms and decorative motifs, Bresnahan also experimented with locally available materials for his ash glazes. He discovered, for example, that elm ash produced a shiny semitransparent glaze but required kiln temperatures in excess of 2,280° centigrade to properly flux.

Although the first glaze chamber of the Takigama kiln easily reached those levels, the back rows of the second and third chambers did not. To solve this problem, Francis Schellinger began carefully segregating the types of wood he used for heating his house and then gave the pure ash to Bresnahan. Basswood ash, Bresnahan soon learned, fluxed at about 2,170° centigrade and thus proved suitable for pots in the kiln's second and third glaze chambers. It was also from Schellinger that Bresnahan first received pure oak ash, which yielded a soft yellow color. In his unending quest for decorative glazes, Bresnahan visited Cargill's Multi-Seed Processing and Refining Plant in West Fargo in 1982. There, he was given the waste ash from burning the hulls of sunflower seeds in large industrial incinerators. Mixed

Tea bowl (Johanna kiln, glaze chamber), 1995, stoneware with *temmoku* glaze, 2¹⁄₄ in. high. In the 13th century, Japanese monks returned home from China with simple tea bowls decorated with a brown-black glaze known as *temmoku.* The clay slips used for this ware were high in iron, which caused the lustrous orange-brown spots that the Japanese poetically called *kaki,* or persimmon. Bresnahan achieves spectacular *temmoku* glazes by filtering iron stone from raw clay and then mixing it with granite dust and flax-straw ash.
Photograph by Gary Mortensen.

Pitcher **(Johanna kiln, glaze chamber), 1995, stoneware with sunflower-seed hull ash glaze, 11¹/₄ in. high. Borrowing from Western forms, Bresnahan often produces simple, sturdy pitchers. This one has a golden ash glaze.**

Photograph by Gary Mortensen.

with clay, feldspar, and water, this ash results in a golden glaze lightly peppered with iron flecks. A year later, Bresnahan traveled to his family's farm in Casselton, North Dakota, where he gathered ash from burning navy-bean straw. When thinly applied, this milky ash glaze is a nearly transparent blue, and when painted over brown designs made from iron oxides, it turns a rich indigo.

In 1985, Bresnahan found he could create a glossy *temmoku* (black) glaze by combining flax-straw ash with granite dust. Always on the lookout for otherwise unusable industrial waste-products, he went to the Cold Spring Granite Company in nearby Cold Spring, Minnesota. The company routinely crushes flawed granite slabs into poultry grit, and it readily agreed to give Bresnahan the fine granite dust the process also produces.

The vast majority of pots from Bresnahan's studio have been unabashedly utilitarian. He has thrown thousands of small lidded jars for storing spices or condiments and medium jars for honey. Cups, with and without handles, also are part of his ongoing repertoire, as well as a variety of serving bowls and platters. He creates such humble objects, he says, so they can be used on a regular basis. And he hopes his functional pieces, like Japanese tea wares, will become even more beautiful in their owners' eyes as they take on the patina that results from frequent handling.

Teapot (Johanna kiln, front fire chamber), 1997, stoneware with natural ash glaze, 7 1/8 in. high. Reed handle by Paul Krueger. Although influenced by traditional Asian forms, Bresnahan freely experiments to improve them functionally and aesthetically. The downturned spout of this teapot prevents drips, while the small feet and thinly potted bottom help cool the tea leaves after the initial brewing so they can be infused for a second and third time. The handle, woven by sculptor Paul Krueger, is far sturdier than ceramic ones, which can easily chip and break.
Photograph by Gary Mortensen.

While Bresnahan derived some of his standard forms from Japan, others came from Europe and America. For instance, he remains particularly fond of sturdy pitchers with handles, long used in the West for everything from water to wine. Occasionally, he also tries to improve traditional wares for both functional and aesthetic reasons. A lover of green tea, he began experimenting with the teapot form in 1982. He found that by turning the spout downward, the liquid did not drip or dribble down the outside of the pot. And by attaching small feet and thinly potting the bottom of the vessel, the tea leaves could cool more quickly after the initial brewing

and thus be infused again for a second and third time. Unfettered by traditional Asian and Western prototypes, he also began exploring the artistic interplay between the teapot and its handle. Working with sculptor Paul Krueger, Bresnahan attached multiple lugs in unusual locations on his pots, for which Krueger would then fashion elaborately woven reed handles. Moreover, Krueger's one-of-a-kind handles are far sturdier than ceramic ones, which can be easily chipped and broken.

The enormous interior capacity of the Johanna kiln also has allowed Bresnahan to produce works on a much grander scale than was possible with his first kiln. For the initial firing of the Johanna kiln in 1995, he produced thirty large jars, some forty inches high. He built these pieces using the coil-and-paddle method, a technique he observed in Japan but was never allowed to do himself. Like other members of his family, Takashi's father had produced such storage jars but instead of smoothing away the paddle marks, as was common, he left them as decoration. Inspired by the Nakazatos, Bresnahan carved the necessary paddles for such wares during the intervals between stoking Takashi's kilns and began using them as soon as he returned to the United States. While Bresnahan is aware that his large jars will probably never be utilitarian in America, he does consider their expansive surfaces irresistible "canvases" on which to draw. By dipping his hands in white or iron-rich slip, he "paints" some of the pots by trailing his fingers across them. He leaves others unadorned, allowing the natural ash glazes that occur in the first chamber during firing to lightly veil their rough surfaces. Still others are "decorated" by placing cups and bowls along their shoulders during the loading process. As the fire engulfs the pots, protected areas remain dark while exposed areas take on a varied color palette or an ash glaze from the intense heat of the flames.

In 1997, Bresnahan began thinking about substituting nitride-bonded, silicon-carbide beams for the large carbide shelves normally used as kiln furniture. During a tour of the Kohler Company's production plant in Wisconsin that year, Bresnahan saw such beams being used and learned they were cutting-edge technology and not available commercially. With dogged persistence, he repeatedly asked the Smith-Sharpe Firebrick Supply Company in Minneapolis about purchasing the high-temperature beams for his own studio. Finally in September 2000, just as the Johanna kiln was being loaded for its fifth firing, he received two of them, each cut into three pieces. In turn, he carefully positioned the sections inside the kiln to act as a framework within which he could tumble stack his ceramics. This open structure enables the heat and flame to travel up and down the pots without being blocked by the traditional solid shelves of the kiln.

Bresnahan's innovative use of recent technology will undoubtedly lead him in new directions. His ongoing quest for new materials also causes him to make unusual discoveries. Most recently, he experimented with a fine, powdery quartz silica from southern Minnesota. After mixing it with a wood ash, he dipped tea bowls in the solution and inadvertently created a dynamic crawling effect in white. Such surprising outcomes have kept Bresnahan, now 48, enthralled with his craft. With his reputation firmly established and his relationship with Saint John's University on solid footing, he continues to develop a regional style that weds his Japanese training with his Midwestern heritage. And through it all, he has remained true to himself and his own unique artistry.

Tea bowl (Johanna kiln, glaze chamber), 1999, stoneware with quartz silica and straw ash glaze, 3 7/8 in. high. Recently, Bresnahan began experimenting with a fine, powdery quartz silica from southern Minnesota. After mixing it with a wood ash, he dipped this tea bowl in the solution and inadvertently created the dynamic crawling effect seen here.
Photograph by Gary Mortensen.

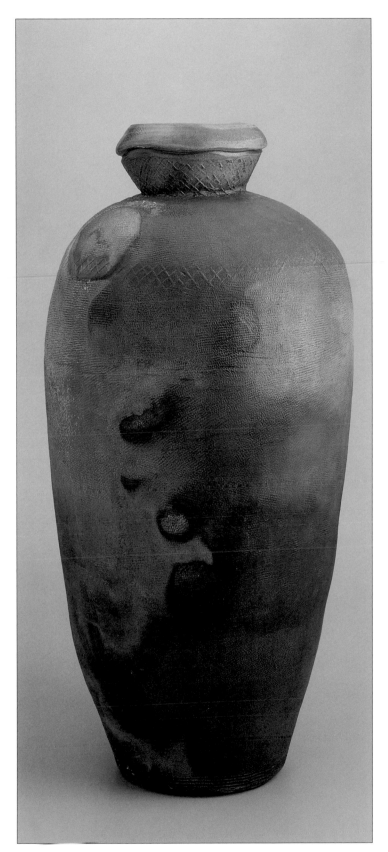

Large jar (Johanna kiln, Tanegashima chamber), 1995, coiled-and-paddled stoneware, 40 in. high.
Photograph by Gary Mortensen.

A Stranger in a Strange Land

The Japanese apprentices heard the American screaming and cursing from down the hillside. Kimura had just returned to the studio after giving the newcomer instructions on how to take a *furo*, a Japanese-style bath. Mostly through hand gestures, he had explained to undress, squat next to the steaming tub, and ladle water over oneself. After completely washing and rinsing, then one could climb into the hot water for a long soak.

The makeshift bathroom was outdoors, surrounded by sheets of corrugated metal with a tarp for a door. Nakazato Takashi's pottery studio had not been finished yet, and it would still be a few weeks before the apprentices' new bathroom could be tiled. In the meantime, they were making use of an old, cast-iron tub. Heated from below by a small fire, the huge caldronlike vat was deep enough for a grown person to sit upright and be completely submerged.

Square dish with five feet (Johanna kiln, front fire chamber), 2000, stoneware with natural ash glaze, 4 1/8 in. high.

Photograph by Gary Mortensen.

Opposite page: While apprenticing in Japan, Bresnahan was invited to participate in Karatsu's annual Okunchi festival. Held in the fall, the festival celebrates a bountiful harvest from the land and the sea. Here, Bresnahan helps pull one of the massive wooden floats through the streets and down to the shore.
November 1976.

Incense containers (Johanna kiln, front fire chamber), 1997, stoneware with natural ash glaze, 2½ in. high (each). Japanese tea masters use a great variety of small ceramic and lacquer containers to hold incense. Bresnahan created this series in that tradition, finishing each small lid uniquely to give the boxes distinct personalities.
Photograph by Gary Mortensen.

On first seeing it, Richard Bresnahan had thought of cartoons of British explorers being boiled alive while Aborigines danced gleefully around. Still, it had been a hot August day and he needed a bath, so he listened carefully to Kimura's instructions.

Once alone, he removed the large wooden lid and grate that floated on the water's surface. After washing, he lowered his body into the steaming vat. His feet slid down the tub's smooth rounded sides. Then, he felt the searing pain—the iron bottom was blisteringly hot. He struggled to get out but was unable to heave himself over the tub's high rim without using his feet. Finally, he kicked off the bottom, let out a yelp, and flopped onto the surrounding wooden platform. There he stood, naked, staring down at his scalded feet when a wide-eyed Kimura tore back the curtain. One look at Bresnahan's bright red soles—and anguished face—and Kimura ran back down the hill, bellowing to the other apprentices for help.

Later, after several cups of rice wine and amid laughter, Kimura apologized for having forgotten to tell Bresnahan not to remove the wooden grate, which was supposed to be pushed down into the water with one's feet to protect them from the caldron's fiery bottom. Once Bresnahan's burns healed, however, the evening *furo* would become his salvation. After a day of intense

Shortly after his arrival in Japan, Bresnahan participated in the firing of Koyama Fujio's final works. At that time, he met Koyama's son Shin'ichi (left) and apprentices Noguchi Koji (center) and Ōoka Akeme.
October 1975.

physical labor around the studio, he soothed his aching back and sore muscles in the relaxing bath, and his frustrations would dissipate like the steam rising off the water's surface. In winter, it provided a welcome refuge from Kyushu's bone-chilling dampness.

In many ways, Richard Bresnahan's experience with the *furo* exemplifies his time in Japan. With its complex social dynamics and strong traditions, Japanese culture was not easy to penetrate, and Bresnahan's initial attempts to do so often resulted in painful disappointment. All he knew about pottery and the skill he had attained from three years of study in Minnesota seemed to be of little consequence in Japan. But most challenging of all—and the source of endless difficulties—was the Japanese language itself. During his first year, especially, he constantly struggled to comprehend what was being said and to make himself understood. The language barrier also created a crushing sense of isolation and loneliness.

***Gourd-shaped teapot* (Johanna kiln, front fire chamber), 1998, stoneware with natural ash glaze, 6¹/₈ in. high. Reed handle by Paul Krueger. For his teapots, Bresnahan collaborates with sculptor Paul Krueger, who fashions handles for the pots from natural materials. Krueger overcame the challenge presented by the small scale and relatively large lid of this vessel by weaving a cantilevered handle, which would not interfere with grasping the lid.**
Photograph by Gary Mortensen.

By his second year, however, having survived countless embarrassing and bewildering situations, he had gained enough facility with the language to be comfortable in most daily encounters. The rewards for his newly acquired proficiency were many, not the least of which was a degree of acceptance in a society traditionally closed to outsiders. And by the time he returned to the United States, Bresnahan had become a profoundly changed person, for Japan had not only permeated his psyche but his very soul.

Japan—Land of Pottery

Despite his studio training at the College of Saint Benedict with Bill Smith and classroom knowledge of Asian ceramics from Sister Johanna Becker, Bresnahan was a neophyte when he arrived in Japan. Like other Americans of his time, he was familiar with the works of such Japanese artists as Hamada Shōji and Kawai Kanjirō. And because of Sister Johanna's diligence, he had been apprised of nearly every book on Japanese ceramics in English, including *The World of Japanese Ceramics* (1967) by Herbert Sanders, *Kenzan and His Tradition* (1966) and *A Potter's Book* (1962) by Bernard Leach, *Tamba Pottery* (1970) and *Kilns* (1973) by Daniel Rhodes, and *Shōji Hamada* (1974) by Susan Peterson.

However, exposure to Asian pottery and techniques through slide lectures and books could not prepare Bresnahan for the reality of Japan's thriving ceramic culture. "For potters," writes the scholar Frederick Baekeland, "the West is a desert, Japan is their oasis"

Nakazato Takashi's wife, Kuniko, preparing a New Year's banquet in her kitchen. The Nakazatos frequently invited important collectors and dealers who visited Karatsu to their home for elaborate meals. Bresnahan was present on such occasions and through them learned a great deal about Japanese cuisine.

Tea bowl (Johanna kiln, Tanegashima chamber, sagger fired), 2000, porcelain with quartz silica and basswood ash glaze, 3½ in. high, 5⅛ in. diameter.
Photograph by Gary Mortensen.

"Sunflower" jar (Johanna kiln, front fire chamber), 1998, stoneware with natural ash glaze, 18 7/8 in. high. To fire this large jar, Bresnahan placed it on its side at the center of the first chamber of the Johanna kiln, near the ceiling. During firing, the heat rebounded off the arch overhead, blasting the upward face of the jar and creating the spectacular sunflower design seen here.
Photograph by Gary Mortensen.

Kensui (Johanna kiln, front fire chamber), 1997, stoneware with natural ash glaze, 7 7/8 in. diameter. During the tea ceremony, the host washes and warms each tea bowl before serving the guest and cleans it again afterward. Low, broad-mouthed containers like this hold the discarded wash water and are called *kensui*.
Photograph by Gary Mortensen.

(Baekeland, *Modern Japanese Ceramics*, p. 15). But what impressed Bresnahan most when he lived in Japan was the extent to which ceramics permeate everyday life. A simple meal, for example, involves a surprising array of small plates and bowls for each person, with individual servings arranged on separate plates in the kitchen beforehand. Even when communal "hot pot" dishes are prepared at the table, people still have their own rice bowl, soup bowl, and a variety of dishes for sauces, pickles, and vegetables. For elaborate meals, dozens of dishes may be placed before a guest over the course of an evening, each vessel holding a carefully prepared and artfully arranged portion. Moreover, each bowl and dish would be different from the surrounding ones—specifically chosen to accord well with the food placed on it.

Bresnahan not only became aware of the sheer quantity of dishes used for meals but learned that housewives in even ordinary homes varied their ceramics according to the season and the occasion. Porcelain plates and bowls with cobalt designs or celadon glazes, for instance, are common in summer, their glassy surfaces and cool hues providing a refreshing visual respite from the heat. In contrast, unglazed stonewares with warm earth tones and soft textures are more appropriate for fall and winter.

In addition, specific foods dictate the type of ceramic utilized. Grilled fish, for example, is usually served on long rectangular plates. Deep, bell-shaped bowls with lids hold soups and stews, whereas straight-sided, flat-bottomed cups contain dipping sauces for soba noodles. A great variety of vessels for dispensing liquids also exists, as well as a surprising number of cups—from the diminutive tumblers used for strong rice wine to the oversized mugs for hot green tea found in sushi restaurants. As a consequence, the humblest kitchens in Japan have veritable stockpiles of ceramics, with every nook and cranny filled to capacity. These Japanese customs radically differ from the European and American preference for matched sets, which are used throughout the year for all foods and on every occasion.

But nowhere is the Japanese reverence for ceramics more evident than in the tea ceremony. As the preparation and serving of powdered green tea became formalized by early Japanese tea masters during the 15th and 16th centuries, a desire to make each occasion unique also arose—an idea implicit in the phrase *ichigo ichie*, "one time, one meeting." To achieve this, tea masters staged *chaji* (tea gatherings) at different times of the day, in different seasons, and with different guests.

Beyond the fluid grace of their ritualized movements in preparing tea, tea masters also demonstrated their artistry through the ceramics, tea implements, and artworks they chose for each gathering. Their carefully considered combinations of objects, known as *toriawase*, revealed their sensitivity to the season and their knowledge of their guests' interests and tastes. Of course, to repeatedly create novel ceremonies and thoughtfully vary the objects they used, tea masters and tea enthusiasts alike voraciously collected pottery and patronized ceramic studios, a practice that continues to this day.

Admittedly, the majority of ceramics found in average Japanese households are mass-produced, commercial-

Rectangular plate (Johanna kiln, Tanegashima chamber), 1999, stoneware with iron slip painting, 9 1/4 in. wide. Photograph by Gary Mortensen.

Tea bowl (Johanna kiln, glaze chamber), 1995, stoneware with navy-bean straw ash glaze, 2 1/2 in. high, 5 1/8 in. diameter. Photographs by Gary Mortensen.

grade porcelains, mechanically decorated and glazed. Nevertheless, most Japanese have a widespread awareness of and admiration for their country's past ceramic traditions, as well as a desire to reference famous styles by the pieces they own. Many people, in fact, possess at least a few historic objects, treasured and passed down from generation to generation, and an astonishing number, especially tea-ceremony enthusiasts, collect works by contemporary potters. Depending on their pocketbooks, they may buy relatively inexpensive studio wares or costly pieces by established artists with national reputations. Many individuals of limited means have even managed to obtain pots by famous contemporary artists by restricting their purchases to more modest objects. In a casual conversation with a

taxi driver in Tokyo, for example, Bresnahan mentioned he apprenticed in a pottery studio in Karatsu. To Bresnahan's amazement, the driver excitedly revealed that he collected tea bowls by one of the country's "Living National Treasures"—Arakawa Toyozō.

Moreover, Bresnahan's arrival in Japan coincided with a national ceramic boom of unprecedented proportions. By the mid-1970s, the Japanese economy had recovered from the devastating effects of the Second World War and was gaining momentum. And potters, like other traditional craftsmen and artists, began to find lucrative markets among an increasingly affluent population. Shortly after his arrival in Karatsu, Bresnahan accompanied Takashi to a pottery exhibition in Soya hosted by a large insurance

Fluted bowl (Johanna kiln, glaze chamber), 1995, stoneware with navy-bean straw ash glaze, 10^1/$_2$ in. diameter.
Photograph by Gary Mortensen.

Flat-sided bottle (Johanna kiln, glaze chamber), 1995,
stoneware with white slip and iron painting under a navy-
bean straw ash glaze, 10 1/2 in. high.
Photograph by Gary Mortensen.

company there. The prices for the works on display (a fraction of what such objects cost today) amazed Bresnahan. "There were a couple of tea bowls for $1,100," he wrote in his journal at the time, "and Koyama Fujio's pieces from the recent firing were going for $60 for a sake cup and $900 for a tea cup. I can see why potters don't starve here."

But other factors beside the economy led to this resurgence. In 1947, the Japan Folk Art Museum, established in 1936 by Yanagi Sōetsu, reopened after a wartime hiatus and exhibited historical works alongside pottery by such 20th-century *mingei* (folk art) artists as Hamada Shōji, Kawai Kanjirō, and Munakata Shikō. By the early 1950s, art organizations like Nitten (Nihon Bijutsu Tenrankai) and the Japan Crafts Society also helped to reestablish ceramics in the national psyche by including traditional pottery in their juried exhibitions. And in 1955, the Japanese government, motivated by the pervasive sentiment that the country's artistic heritage was being lost in the wake of rampant industrialization, instigated a system of naming individuals as "Holders of Important Intangible Cultural Properties," or "Living National Treasures" as they have become known (Baekeland, "Modern Japanese Studio Ceramics," p. 22). Shortly after Bresnahan's arrival in Japan, in fact, Nakazato Tarōuemon XII (Muan), Takashi's father and the retired head of the Nakazato studio in Karatsu, received this coveted honor and the sudden international fame and monetary rewards that resulted from it.

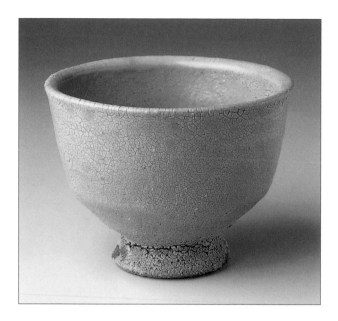

Tea bowl (Johanna kiln, glaze chamber), 1999, stoneware with quartz silica and elm ash glaze, 4 in. high, 5¹/₄ in. diameter.
Photograph by Gary Mortensen.

Melon bowl (Johanna kiln, Tanegashima chamber), 1998, stoneware, 10¹/₂ in. diameter. The Japanese serve food in a variety of unmatched bowls and plates that are meant to be picked up while eating. Consequently, part of the meal's enjoyment comes from the visual and tactile "feast" provided by the ceramics themselves. This small serving bowl reflects that tradition and has the delicate lobed shape of a young melon.
Photograph by Gary Mortensen.

During the 1960s, museum exhibitions further validated the ceramist's standing within the art world and provided collectors with unbiased information about numerous potters. The Kyoto National Museum of Modern Art held the earliest of these exhibits, "A View of Contemporary Japanese Ceramics," in 1963. The following year, Koyama Fujio organized "Contemporary International Ceramics" at the Tokyo National Museum of Modern Art. In addition to works by Japan's finest potters, he included pieces by nineteen non-Japanese artists. And in 1968, another exhibition at the Kyoto National Museum of Modern Art, "A New Generation of Contemporary Ceramics," attempted to circumvent the politics of the established art organizations, which consistently promoted their most senior members, by requiring that the exhibited pieces be made by potters who were less than fifty years old (Nakanodō, "Japanese Public Collections," pp. 62–63).

In turn, the marketplace responded to this burgeoning public awareness of contemporary ceramics. Japanese department stores, together with major news organizations, also began to host ceramic exhibitions. The stores profited by increased foot traffic, and the newspapers by rising circulation among the art-going public, as well as from the sale of exhibition catalogues, postcards, and posters (Baekeland, "Modern Japanese Studio Ceramics," p. 16). Takashi, for example, had showings of his works at such prestigious department stores as Mitsukoshi and Seibu in Tokyo and Takashimaya in Osaka.

Vase (Johanna kiln, front fire chamber), 1997, stoneware with natural ash glaze, 10 in. high. To form this vase, Bresnahan first threw a straight-sided cylinder and cut the surface with wire to create facets. Then, using one hand, he shaped it again from the inside, causing the vertical facets to twist.

Photograph by Gary Mortensen.

In addition to department store exhibitions, private galleries specializing in contemporary ceramics also opened. Galleries hosted both solo exhibitions and group shows and sometimes based their installations on a common theme, like tea bowls, flower vases, or daily wares (*shoki-no-mono*). For potters, whose studios tended to be in rural locations, gallery representation in metropolitan areas became the best outlet for marketing their works. The Mune Kōgei Gallery in Ginza and the Green Gallery in Asakusa, for example, hosted exhibitions of Takashi's works from the first firing (*hatsugama*) of his Karatsu kiln in 1976.

To be immersed in a culture that so obviously valued ceramics and their makers greatly contributed to Bresnahan's initial euphoria in Japan. However, as time went on, he also became aware of the rapacious nature of the Japanese art market. Department store managers and gallery owners aggressively lobbied Takashi for his best works, and heated arguments sometimes occurred between dealers over certain pieces while the pottery was still being unloaded from the kiln. In addition, Bresnahan saw the unrelenting pressure to create a steady stream of work for the marketplace. When Takashi was in Karatsu, the pace was inhumanly frantic, and even though the wood-burning kiln was fired three times a year and the gas kiln nearly every month, demand often outstripped

Canister (Johanna kiln, front fire chamber), 1995, stoneware with natural ash glaze, 13½ in. high. Bresnahan's tall canisters can function as *mizusashi* (fresh water jars) during a tea ceremony or, without their lids, as sturdy vases.
Photograph by Gary Mortensen.

the studio's ability to produce. Takashi was also expected to attend numerous exhibition openings in Tokyo, Nagoya, Kyoto, and Osaka. And while good relations with gallery owners ensured financial prosperity, success came at a high personal cost and often led to a distancing from the surrounding community as the potter's wares became expensive commodities for the national and international art market.

At the same time, Bresnahan never lost sight of the vast difference between Japanese attitudes and American ones. In the United States, potters struggle to survive in a market that places little value on functional handmade ceramics. But in Japan, there is a widespread affection for a preindustrial system in which potters and other craftsmen make goods largely for their local communities. To honor and maintain that tradition, Bresnahan has always had an open-door policy at his Saint John's studio. He leads an astonishing number of tours, patiently explaining how clay and glazes are processed, how pots are thrown, and how the massive Johanna kiln works. Individual visitors to the studio often find him at the wheel or gently scraping kiln debris off his fired pots. True to his Japanese experience, he is quick to offer a cup of tea and initiate a lively conversation about the merits of handmade ceramics. Ultimately, he believes the sale of a pot is more about conveying the philosophy behind its creation than about its price. Japan also proved to him that even in one of the most industrialized nations on earth, handmade pottery could play a vital role in daily life. Whereas the Japanese still strongly relate to the aesthetic traditions of their country before its late 19th-century modernization, Americans lack such an empathy with their past. And

Bresnahan fully understood that the enduring popularity of ceramics in Japan stemmed from their basic utilitarian function, both in everyday life and the rarefied atmosphere of the tearoom.

He realized that if he were to succeed as a potter in the United States, he, too, would need to create pieces that were pertinent to American life. For this reason, he seldom makes *chawan* (wide-mouthed tea bowls)— possibly the most loved and scrutinized of all Japanese ceramics—because they have little relevance to the American lifestyle. But given our predilection for communal dining, he often produces large serving bowls and platters. Moreover, he has freely adapted some Japanese forms to suit American needs. Shortly after his return to the Midwest, for example, he developed a tall canister shape loosely based on bronze sutra containers. An artful alternative to plastic or metal kitchen canisters, Bresnahan's storage jars can hold sugar, flour, and other foodstuffs. But their elegant proportions also allow them to be flower vases.

Early on, Bresnahan also discovered a demand for generously proportioned single-serving bowls with lids. In Japan, such covered bowls are used for *donburi*, a rice dish topped with seasoned egg and chicken. But here, they work well for heating individual servings in microwave ovens—the lid preventing spatters and later converting to a bread plate. And in general, Bresnahan found he needed to increase the overall scale of his pots to match the greater physical size of most Americans. Many of his customers, for example, liked the feel of his handleless Asian-style teacups, but preferred 16-ounce vessels to the smaller 8-to-10-ounce Japanese ones.

"Passing Moon" jar (Johanna
kiln, Tanegashima chamber),
1997, stoneware, 27 1/8 in.
high.
Photograph by Gary Mortensen.

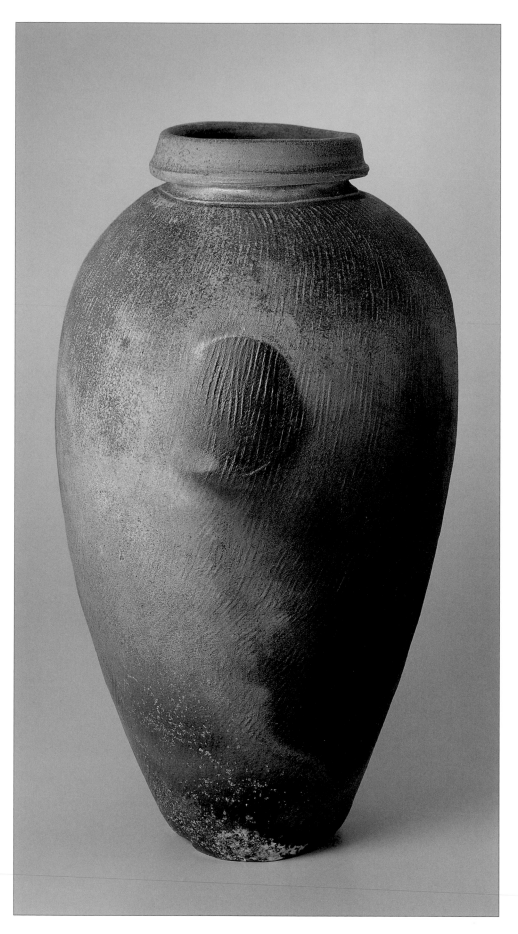

Bottle (Johanna kiln, Tanegashima
chamber), 1999, stoneware with
salt-glazed neck, 7 in. high.
Photograph by Gary Mortensen.

The Potter and Nature

The risk of fire from wood-burning kilns has long forced Japanese potters to locate their studios away from densely populated areas. Out in the countryside, they make their livelihoods alongside farmers and like them have existences closely tied to seasonal cycles.

Because summer rains create pools of water on level fields with underground deposits of nonpermeable materials, that is the best time of year to find clay. The rain-soaked ground also makes for easier excavation. But summer's oppressive heat and humidity can impede a kiln's drafting ability, so firings are usually held in spring and autumn. (Winter makes unloading the kiln and washing the wares tortuously cold.) Autumn is also the season when potters gather straw ash for their glazes, after the grain has been harvested and the remaining stalks and leaves have been burned.

Of course, the potter's most direct link to the natural world starts with the clay itself. Japanese potters, in fact, base their production on the very nature of local clays, and many would never work with preprocessed materials from manufacturers as most Americans do. Indeed, their paramount concern is with the *tsuchi-aji*, the "taste" or personality of the clay. Whenever Japanese potters gather, the conversation inevitably turns to the clay they each use and its characteristics, how it impacts the forms they create, and how it fires. Whenever they discuss an old ceramic, they invariably turn it over to examine its unglazed foot. Is the grain rough or smooth? Has the firing left it brownish red or tan, suggesting a higher or lower iron content? Did the potter utilize the innate qualities of the clay or does the pot have structural weaknesses?

Needless to say, most Japanese potters devote tremendous energy and resources to obtaining local clay and processing it. Takashi, for example, typically stockpiled a five-year supply of raw clay on site, which was kept in a massive concrete box adjoining the storage building. This centuries-old loyalty to indigenous materials undoubtedly began with the realities of rural life. "Within the cultural and administrative enclaves that made up the totality of Japan," writes the scholar Daniel Rhodes, "the artist and craftsman worked in relative isolation from his counterparts in the rest of the country. Because of the impracticability of long-distance transportation, local raw materials were relied upon almost exclusively. Local pride and provincial conservatism encouraged a persistence in local ways and styles, and a relative indifference to influences from the outside" (Rhodes, *Tamba Pottery*, p. 13).

While this was certainly true during Japan's medieval era, improved roads had greatly increased communication between provinces by the late 16th century. Tea masters during the Edo period also were familiar with various rustic wares and liked using them with more refined objects during the tea ceremony. And given the era's rampant mercantilism, it seems likely that if a potter (or his patron) wanted clays, glaze materials, or pigments from a different region, they could have been obtained. So beyond their remote locations, Japanese potters consciously fostered a commitment to local resources that not only transcended the materials' inherent shortcomings and idiosyncrasies but celebrated them.

This approach undoubtedly stems from the Japanese love of nature and the tendency to ascribe an independent integrity—even divinity—to the natural world. The earliest form of religious worship in Japan, Shinto, or "way of the gods," recognized mountains, ancient trees, waterfalls, and other natural phenomena as sanctums for supernatural beings known as *kami*. This belief, coupled with the country's natural beauty, hospitable topography, and temperate climate, engendered in the Japanese a palpable intimacy with nature. From that viewpoint, clay was not something to be subjugated by the potter but a divine manifestation of nature worthy of admiration and respect.

This creative partnership with the natural world extends to the act of wood firing itself. As early as the 15th and 16th centuries, color variations and distortions caused by the raging fire—as it engulfs the vessels, leaving glassy rivulets of ash glazes on them and sometimes warping them—have been admired as nature's unique contribution to the potter's art. Even when potters try to induce such effects by the way they load the kilns and the fuels they use, there are always elements of chance outside their control. Similarly, Japanese potters—and tea masters—have always accepted the unavoidable blemishing that occurs from stacking pots in the kiln as part of their inherent aesthetics. "I spent my first day of vacation cleaning the small plates with a chisel," wrote Bresnahan during his Japanese apprenticeship, "taking off the clay wads that had been used to stack the pottery and chipping away anything remaining on the insides of the plates. In America, I believe they are called scars; in Japan, they are considered accent marks, something that enhances. What a nice way to think of them."

Small bowls in the style of Nakazato Takashi (Takashi's Ryūtagama gas kiln), 1978, stoneware with feldspathic wood ash glaze over Korean kaolin slip, 2 3/4 in. high (each). Following Takashi's example, Bresnahan made these elegant bowls while he was in Japan. They derive their shape from the open pod of a Japanese peppercorn.
Photograph by Gary Mortensen.

Tall bottle with three lugs (Johanna kiln, Tanegashima chamber), 1997, stoneware with natural ash glaze, 14 7/8 in. high.
Photograph by Gary Mortensen.

Bresnahan was also struck by how much contemporary potters still depend on the natural world for their artistic inspiration. Karatsu potters, for example, have decorated their wares with simplified images of native plants and animals for generations and continue to do so. Once, Takashi even went a step further when he based a small bowl (*mukozuke*) on the organic shape of a Japanese peppercorn (*sanshō*) pod.

"Today was my day of enlightenment," wrote Bresnahan in November 1975. "It was later in the afternoon, and *sensei* was beginning to throw an unusual form, but it seemed to have no functional value. So I stopped my work, walked over, and watched him do fifteen or so. . . . After setting one of the forms on the board, *sensei* opened the drawer next to him and pulled out a bunch of [what looked like] small dried flowers. He broke one off, looked at it for a second, and then gave it to me. There were three black seeds being protected by three small cups no bigger than my smallest fingernail. I looked at the small weed ready to send its seeds to the wind and the form on the wheel and my mouth almost dropped into the clay."

Ceramics and the Tea Ceremony

As part of Bresnahan's apprenticeship, Takashi encouraged him to attend tea ceremonies at the Nakazato family compound in Karatsu hosted by Tarōuemon XIII's wife, a certified tea master. In addition to her regular students—mostly women from the surrounding community—members of Tarōuemon's studio and Takashi's had a standing invitation to participate as their work schedules permitted. After these gatherings, Bresnahan's knees and ankles would ache miserably for hours. Nor could he escape his own feelings of being awkward and self-conscious during these graceful rituals. Nonetheless, these ceremonies exerted a lasting influence on Bresnahan's life and development as an artist.

A typical lesson began with the participants meeting in the waiting room adjacent to the tearoom. After exchanging hushed greetings, the tea master would signal for them to enter the tearoom. One by one, they would proceed to the *tokonoma*, an alcove for the display of an artwork or simple flower arrangement, and then take their places in the tearoom. For the next hour, they would sit quietly on bent knees, carefully observing Mrs. Nakazato's elegance and precision as she prepared a bowl of tea for each of them. The solemn stillness of the room was broken only by the sounds of pouring water, the soft scrape of the bamboo whisk against the inside of the tea bowl, and the codified

Minneapolis tea master Patricia Katagiri examining one of Bresnahan's tea bowls.
Photograph by James R. Dean, December 2000.

exchange between the master and the guests as she placed the prepared tea before them. After serving everyone, Mrs. Nakazato would replenish the water in the kettle and carefully rinse and wipe each bowl. Then, she would place the lacquered tea caddy (*natsume*) and the bamboo scoop (*chashaku*) before the guests for their examination. At that time, she would also answer any questions they had about her selections, the pots and their makers, and if the pieces had any notable provenances or poetic titles. Before quietly leaving, the participants would once again contemplate the display in the *tokonoma*.

Tea bowl (Johanna kiln, Tanegashima chamber, sagger fired), 1998, porcelain with elm ash glaze over iron painting, 3¹/₄ in. high, 4¹/₄ in. diameter. Bresnahan usually fires glazed ware in the second chamber of the Johanna kiln for eight to ten hours. Recently, however, he has begun placing some glazed pots in protective clay boxes known as saggers and firing them for five-and-a-half days in the Tanegashima chamber. This prolonged exposure to intense heat causes elm ash glaze, which typically is transparent, to blush blue, white, and yellow.
Photograph by Gary Mortensen.

Tea ceremony aesthetics have strongly influenced Bresnahan's style. Here, Carin Manbeck of Minneapolis prepares tea using one of his tea bowls and a *mizusashi* (fresh water jar). Photograph by James R. Dean, December 2000.

More elaborate gatherings included a specially prepared meal (*kaiseki*). After dining, guests drank a thick tea (*koicha*), prepared with three scoops of powdered tea for each bowl, and then a thin tea (*usucha*), made with only one scoop. Occasions like these, which lasted for several hours, gave each participant the chance to see an even wider array of tea utensils and ceramics.

The Nakazatos did not arrange for these classes with the idea their apprentices would one day become tea masters. Rather, they hoped to instill in them a proper regard for ceramics and their handling. Objects used in tea ceremonies are accorded special respect, and the humility with which each guest receives a bowl of tea has been likened to the proper deportment of a Zen monk, whose sustenance depends on the generosity of others. After drinking, each person leans forward to closely examine the tea bowl. With elbows resting on knees, they hold their bowls with both hands, only a few centimeters above the tatami flooring. In this way, if someone accidentally dropped the bowl, it probably would not be damaged. Similarly, participants always

Mizusashi (Johanna kiln, Tanegashima chamber), 1998, stoneware, 7 1/2 in. high. The opaque velvety surfaces of pieces from the Tanegashima chamber of the Johanna kiln can make the pots appear dense and somewhat ponderous. To counter this effect, Bresnahan often puts small feet on his vessels to lighten them visually. The fluttering, skirtlike sides of this *mizusashi* (water jar) also give the impression of weightlessness. Photograph by Gary Mortensen.

Mizusashi (Johanna kiln, front fire chamber), 1997, stoneware with sunflower-seed hull ash glaze, 8 3/8 in. high. *Mizusashi* (water jars) hold fresh water for replenishing the kettle during the tea ceremony. Bresnahan learned to make these forms during his apprenticeship in Japan, and he now creates a few each year to accommodate the growing popularity of *chanoyu* (tea ceremony) in the United States.
Photograph by Gary Mortensen.

remove their rings and other jewelry before a tea ceremony to prevent the tea bowls from becoming chipped or scratched.

Usually, at such gatherings, antique wares are also brought out for careful scrutiny and their aesthetics discussed. How had the vessel been shaped? How did the maker trim the foot? How was the glaze applied? In fact, Bresnahan soon realized that his perception of a work always changed once he had held it and that the success of any bowl depended on how it felt in the hands. Somber hued and generously proportioned pieces that appeared to be heavily potted, for example, were often surprisingly light and comfortable to hold. And the subtle texture of

Karatsu's sandy clay, veiled by a thin layer of glaze, was pleasingly tactile and soft to the touch.

By attending tea ceremonies, potters could determine which forms worked best for their intended purpose. During one tea gathering, Bresnahan learned the jars that hold fresh water (*mizusashi*) are often bulky in shape because, unlike tea bowls, they are meant to be viewed from across the room. Vases hung on the *tokobashira* (main pillar) of the *tokonoma* often taper toward the bottom, so they visually blend with the wood instead of jutting out from it. And bright overglaze enamels occurred most often on small objects, like incense boxes, which prevented them from becoming too ostentatious within the subtle confines of the tearoom.

Born and raised in Tokoname, Koie Ryoji has fashioned clay his entire life—first as a factory worker and then as an artist. As a young man, he lost two of his fingers in a factory accident. He gouges the surfaces of his pots, he says, because psychologically he is still hunting for his missing fingers.
Photograph by James R. Dean, April 1998.

Moreover, Bresnahan became aware that the tea master's reverence for antique objects even included the way they were stored. Some objects had hand-made brocade bags, precious in their own right, and specially constructed wooden boxes. Particularly prized pieces often had multiple boxes, the lids inscribed with laudatory phrases written by past tea masters and owners. Other objects had poetic names or titles inspired by the moods they invoked in their possessors. Bresnahan marveled at how "alive" these ceramics continued to be. They were not merely relics, stodgy with age and unrelated to modern life, but works of art whose beauty only increased with time and handling. Even objects that somehow had become chipped or broken had been skillfully mended with gold lacquer—the breaks themselves becoming part of the innate character of the piece and its accrued history.

Beyond Karatsu

Without question, Richard Bresnahan's development as an artist owes an enormous debt to his teacher, Nakazato Takashi, and the Nakazato family of potters in Karatsu. From processing raw clay and formulating glazes to constructing kilns and mastering the *hera* and the Karatsu-style kick wheel, they taught him well. And had his experience in Japan been limited to their studios alone, it would have been a rich one indeed.

But during Bresnahan's three-and-a-half-year apprenticeship, he occasionally traveled beyond Karatsu and its environs. Sometimes, he went with Takashi and at other times, alone. These outings enabled him to explore other Japanese ceramic traditions and meet a diverse group of potters. The friendships he forged during these intense encounters have been some of the most enduring and nourishing of his career.

In many ways, Japan was a good place for potters to be in the 1970s and early eighties. With interest in contemporary ceramics booming, Japanese students could realistically consider a career as a potter instead of one as a corporate "salaryman." Japan's traditional production areas also provided economic stability and grew in population as aspiring young potters went in search of apprenticeships. While some began their studies in newly created university or technical school programs, most finished their instruction in an established studio with a master who taught them age-old methods and forms. Not surprisingly, these apprenticeships were not merely exclusive but somewhat secretive (Cort, "Portrait of a Moment," pp. 18–19).

"Technical knowledge, deeply cultivated on the local level," writes scholar Louise Cort, "was not shared between centers, and many workshops still guarded

their techniques from their neighbors" (Cort, p. 18). Bresnahan recounts in his journal, for example, how once he and Takashi visited another pottery to surreptitiously find out more about salt glazing and how to stave off salt's corrosive effects on the kiln. Before arriving, they decided Takashi would feign disinterest in the subject, thereby disarming his rival, and Bresnahan, as the curious foreigner, would ask seemingly naive questions to get technical details out of the unsuspecting potter.

Despite this persistent reticence among established artists to exchange information, several younger, more progressive individuals began to opt for more open communication during the 1970s. Two of the earliest of these were Koie Ryoji and Kaneko Jun, who organized "Earth Festival" in March 1972. Held in Tokoname, the event made twenty tons of clay available to five hundred participants, who created both avant-garde objects and traditional ones on site.

Koie Ryoji, *Wide-mouthed jar* (Johanna kiln, front fire chamber), 1999, stoneware with natural ash glaze, 15 in. high. During a week-long visit in 1998, Koie made several works at the Saint John's studio, which Bresnahan fired for him the following fall. Inspired by the Johanna kiln's grand scale, Koie coil built four large jars—the first time he had done so in twenty years. After constructing the bottom half of the vessel upside-down, he inverted it into a five-gallon plastic bucket. The line where he joined the upper half of the jar can be seen beneath the pot's swelling shoulders. As he pinched the coils together with his fingers, he left the marks in the clay to give the jar its distinctive texture.
Photograph by Gary Mortensen.

The spectacle of so many potters from all over Japan working side-by-side was both unprecedented and exhilarating. Even Koyama Fujio breached traditional boundaries by freely talking about what he had gleaned over the years, from both excavating old kiln sites and attempting to replicate past ceramic styles (Smith, "Earth Is Alive," pp. 12–13).

Bresnahan first met Kaneko Jun in the summer of 1976, when he and Suzuki Goro arrived at Takashi's studio driving a flatbed truck with a small clapboard house perched on it. Long-haired and in their mid-30s, they were looking for a potter who would make extremely large pots for Kaneko to paint with his intense colors. Kaneko had moved back to Japan in 1975 after teaching at the Rhode Island School of Design. After buying land in Nagura, he had constructed his own house and immense studio using recycled materials. He also had built several gas kilns for his large sculptural works.

His friend Suzuki worked out of a humble studio in Seto and had already become an expert on Japanese clays and

Bresnahan first met Suzuki Goro in Karatsu in 1976. Despite his bohemian lifestyle, the young Suzuki, an expert on clays and glazing materials, was already a superb potter capable of replicating historic ceramics with astonishing accuracy.

Suzuki Goro, *Teapot* (Takigama kiln, front fire chamber), 1982, 10¹⁄₄ in. high. Suzuki and Bresnahan have been friends since they met in Japan in 1976. In 1982, Suzuki visited Minnesota and spent two weeks at Bresnahan's studio, creating a large number of works he asked Bresnahan to finish for him in his next firing. To give this teapot layers of natural glazing to match its expressive shape, Bresnahan fired it on five separate occasions.
Photograph by Gary Mortensen.

Kakutani Mitsuo, *Platter* (Johanna kiln, front fire chamber), 1998, stoneware, 14 1/2 in. high, 14 in. wide. As a painter, Kakutani approaches clay as if it were canvas—inducing expressive surface effects by the way he loads his works in the kiln.
Photograph by Gary Mortensen.

Bresnahan and Kakutani Mitsuo have been close friends and colleagues since they first met in Japan in 1976. Kakutani, a painter who teaches at Earlham College in Indiana, visited Bresnahan frequently during the 1980s and has participated in every firing of the Johanna kiln.

Photograph by James R. Dean, October 1995.

potting materials. A superb technician and artist, Suzuki produced black and yellow Seto, Shino, and Oribe ware with clays and glazes astonishingly similar to historic examples but decorated with his own unique motifs. Deeply impressed with his and Kaneko's far-reaching knowledge of ceramics and radical creativity, Bresnahan stayed up until 4 A.M. talking with them on their first night in Karatsu. Later, he would visit both of them at their own studios.

In turn, Kaneko advised Bresnahan to meet Koie Ryoji, who knew more about wood firing than anyone he had met. Born and raised in Tokoname, Koie had grown up working with factory craftsmen who made clay drainpipes and industrial tile. Then, he studied historic Tokoname ware at the Tokoname Ceramic Research Institute. His vast technical knowledge gave him enormous freedom to experiment artistically. He created avant-garde sculptures, as well as functional platters and vases, from inexpensive industrial clays and fired them in large, multichambered kilns of his own design.

For Bresnahan, Koie epitomized his concept of an artist. Unlike most Japanese ceramists, Koie had no mentor and felt no obligation to follow any of Japan's historical traditions. Instead, against great odds and financial constraints, he had decided to make his own mark creatively and in his own way. A man of inexhaustible energy and good humor, he and his wife had made their humble home a welcoming place for artists of all kinds. He even invited their guests to add their own drawings to his children's, which were playfully scrawled across the house's *fusuma* (sliding doors). During his visit, Bresnahan was so taken by Koie's untrammeled spirit he composed a poem called "Bear's Lair," which likens a wood kiln to a wild bear:

> In winter, the kiln also sleeps
> In spring, she's hungry
> In summer, the bear and the kiln are miserably hot
> In fall, with winter coming, it's time to eat and fire.

Afterward, Koie wrote Bresnahan's verse in Japanese and presented it to him as a memento of their evening together; Bresnahan did the same in English for Koie.

***Bresnahan's "Bear's Lair" poem with calligraphy by Koie Ryoji**, 1978, ink on paper, 25 in. high, 38 1/2 in. wide.*
Photograph by Gary Mortensen.

***Teapot** (Johanna kiln, Tanegashima chamber), 1995, stoneware, 6 1/2 in. high. Reed handle by Paul Krueger.*
Photograph by Gary Mortensen.

Another Japanese potter who inspired Bresnahan with his irrepressible tenacity was Morioka Shigeyoshi. Living in the mountains near Wakayama on the island of Honshū, Morioka had built his own house and studio entirely from materials he had salvaged from a nearby landfill. He also had fashioned a long split-bamboo kiln up the steep hillside, in which he fired an array of daily wares. Bresnahan had first met Morioka in Karatsu when he helped with the first firing of Takashi's *noborigama* in May 1976. As a reciprocal gesture, Takashi had then sent Bresnahan to assist Morioka with his own firing later that same year. Although just at the beginning of his career, Morioka impressed Bresnahan with his free spirit and fierce determination to carve out a life for himself.

But one of the closest and most enduring friendships Bresnahan made in Japan was with Kakutani Mitsuo. An established painter, Kakutani teaches studio art classes in Richmond, Indiana, at Earlham College. After becoming interested in clay by watching Takashi give pottery demonstrations at Earlham, Kakutani traveled throughout Japan one summer, visiting pottery studios. During that trip, he made arrangements to see Takashi and met Bresnahan. The two had instant rapport, and after Bresnahan returned to the Midwest, they developed a lasting social and artistic camaraderie.

During his years in Japan, Bresnahan also came into contact with a surprising number of Westerners. During the 1970s, the Japanese government had set aside funding for the study of traditional culture. That, coupled with the relatively low cost of living, led many foreign students to secure apprenticeships or enter university programs in Japan. Bresnahan met most of these potters when they visited Karatsu or during his own

travels. In all cases, these encounters provided ample opportunity for the rapid exchange of information in English. These acquaintances included an Austrian, Felix Stromehier, who had a studio in Kameoka while his wife attended Bijutsu Daigaku in Kyoto, and several Americans: Donna Gilliss, who studied with Isazaki Jun in Bizen; Joy Brown, who apprenticed with Morioka Shigeyoshi in Wakayama; Paul Chaleff, who was visiting various studios in Japan; and Doug Laurie, an established potter who, after apprenticing with Kawai Kanjirō, still lived in Kameoka in a sprawling samurai house he had restored.

At the same time, Bresnahan came into contact with important American collectors of Japanese art. In 1976, he met Mary Burke, who was visiting Takashi's studio with the curator of her collection, Andrew Pecarik, and Julia Meech, a curator at the Metropolitan Museum of Art in New York City. A few weeks later, he was introduced to Kimiko and John Powers, who invited him to Kyoto to view the annual exhibition of treasures

In the summer of 1977, Bresnahan (top left), together with Joy Brown (top right), Jessie Morioka (lower left), and Paul Chaleff, helped fire Morioka Shigeyoshi's kiln in Wakayama.

Nakazato Takashi fired his *noborigama* in Karatsu around-the-clock for seven days and enlisted the help of other potters. Here, Bresnahan pours sake for Morioka Shigeyoshi (foreground), while Austrian potter Felix Stromehier looks on.

Nakazato Takashi's father, Nakazato Tarōuemon XII, who is known by the art name Muan, became a "Living National Treasure" in Japan in 1976.

Bottle (Johanna kiln, front fire chamber), 2000, stoneware with natural ash glaze, 10¼ in. high.
Photograph by Gary Mortensen.

106

Bresnahan using a sunken Karatsu-style kick wheel at Nakazato Takashi's studio in 1976.

owned by the Daitokuji temple. And that same year at Takashi's exhibition in Ginza at the Mune Kōgei Gallery, he met Sydney Cardozo, one of the earliest foreign collectors of contemporary Japanese ceramics. Before his return to the United States, Bresnahan visited Cardozo at his tiny Tokyo apartment and was amazed while he pulled out piece after piece by such illustrious potters as Arakawa Toyozō and Kitaōji Rosanjin.

All of these experiences did much to broaden Bresnahan's artistic training. Travel to other pottery centers, particularly when he knew people there, greatly enhanced his knowledge of both traditional and modern Japanese ceramics and made him aware of a wide range of potting techniques, firing methods, and kiln types. As significantly, he consorted with potters whose maverick approaches were not merely out of the ordinary but downright infectious. Undaunted by the challenges of daily life, they built their own studios, kilns, and houses using alternative methods that neither compromised their principles nor led to staggering debt. And most importantly, they did it all with great panache, boundless energy, and a conviction worthy of his deepest respect and emulation.

Body and Soul

The potter sits at his work and turns the wheel with his feet; he is always deeply concerned over his work, and perfects his output in detail. He molds the clay with his hands and makes it pliable with his feet; he sets his heart to finish the glazing, and carefully watches the fire in his kiln. All these rely upon their hands, and each is skilled in his own work. Without them a city cannot be established, and no one can sojourn or live there. Yet they are not sought out for the council of the people, nor do they attain eminence in the public assembly. They do not sit in the judge's seat nor are they found among the rulers; they cannot expound discipline or judgment, and they are not found using proverbs. But they keep stable the fabric of the world, and their concern is in the practice of their trade.

—Sirach 38:29–34

In retrospect, it seems inevitable that the young Richard Bresnahan accepted Saint John's invitation to set up a pottery studio on campus. After all, he had gone to school there for many years and was familiar with the local community; he also was from the Midwest, and his immediate family still lived close by in North Dakota.

Opposite page: Bresnahan decorating large bowls at his first studio, which was located in the basement of St. Joseph Hall at Saint John's University.
Photograph by James R. Dean, May 1985.

Father Michael Blecker was so impressed with Bresnahan's experience in Japan and his commitment to using sustainable natural resources that he invited him to be the university's artist-in-residence in 1979.

On October 12, 1994, Abbot Timothy Kelly (middle) blessed the Johanna kiln, Bresnahan's second wood-burning kiln at Saint John's University. Brother Dietrich Reinhart (left) and Brother Paul-Vincent Niebauer also participated in the celebration.

Photograph by Laura A. Crosby, 1994.

Much more surprising is the fact that the offer was ever made in the first place. In 1979, there was no funding for the position, the idea did not exist in any university plan, and Bresnahan was remembered by some faculty as a difficult student. Certainly, Father Michael Blecker, then president of the university, and Father Jerome Theisen, who became abbot of Saint John's Abbey that fall, must have been impressed by the potter's extensive apprenticeship in Japan and charmed by his wild idealism and boundless energy. Perhaps they both also harbored secret hopes that the young man would eventually decide to join their order. But these reasons alone only partially explain Father Michael's determination to make Bresnahan the university's official artist-in-residence. In fact, his decision reflected Benedictine ideals that had shaped the monastery and school since its beginnings in Minnesota in the 1850s.

Bowl (Johanna kiln, glaze chamber), 2000, stoneware with iron painting under a navy-bean straw ash glaze, 6 in. high, 12 in. diameter.

Photograph by Gary Mortensen.

"Global Harmony" platter (Bresnahan's gas kiln), 1995, stoneware with iron painting under a navy-bean straw ash glaze, 20 1/8 in. diameter. In 1995, the St. Paul–Nagasaki Sister City Committee asked Bresnahan to create two platters to commemorate the 50th anniversary of the atomic bombing of Nagasaki, Japan. The committee presented one of the platters to the mayor of Nagasaki and the other one to the mayor of St. Paul, Minnesota. Each vessel bears an inscription on the bottom: a *waka*-style poem by Father Neal Lawrence. Lawrence, who was General Douglas MacArthur's liaison officer during World War II, had been sent to Nagasaki and Hiroshima after the bombings to view the devastation firsthand.

Photograph by Gary Mortensen.

"Prophetic Messenger" platter (Johanna kiln, Tanegashima chamber), 1995, stoneware with slip painting and gold leaf, 13 1/4 in. diameter. When a hunter mistakenly shot a friend's Arabian brood mare, Bresnahan saw the incident as a chilling reminder of our modern disengagement from the natural world. On this platter, he depicted a horse as a divine messenger, an idea common to many cultures. He showed the spirited animal descending on celestial rays and rearing up before an archway that separates the heavens from the earth. The arch itself has symbols representing human greed (money), aggression (missiles), and the natural world (trees and water).

Photograph by Gary Mortensen.

Self-Sufficiency and Industriousness

On May 20, 1856, five Benedictine monks arrived in the Minnesota Territory and the town of St. Cloud. They had been sent west six weeks earlier by Abbot Boniface Wimmer of the Saint Vincent Abbey in Latrobe, Pennsylvania, and told to minister to the growing numbers of German Catholics in the region. After their arduous journey, the young monks must have thought the small settlement on the banks of the Mississippi to be a very remote and wild place. But they also must have been excited knowing they were participating in the rebirth of a religious way of life that had nearly become extinct just a few decades earlier.

Their order had its beginnings in the early sixth century with Benedict (480–544) of Nursia. The son of an aristocratic Umbrian family, Benedict had gone to Rome to study but was so offended by the city's licentiousness that he fled. He found a cave near the ruins of Nero's palace in Subiaco and spent three years there as a hermit. In time, other young men approached him who wanted to emulate his devotion and self-discipline. Believing a Christian life of worship and work was best practiced in communities, he responded to their entreaties by forming small groups of twelve monks each. In 529, he journeyed south with a band of disciples and arrived at the town of Cassino, halfway between Rome and Naples. There, on a remote mountaintop, he established the monastery that bears his name and wrote the regulations that governed the brotherhood's existence.

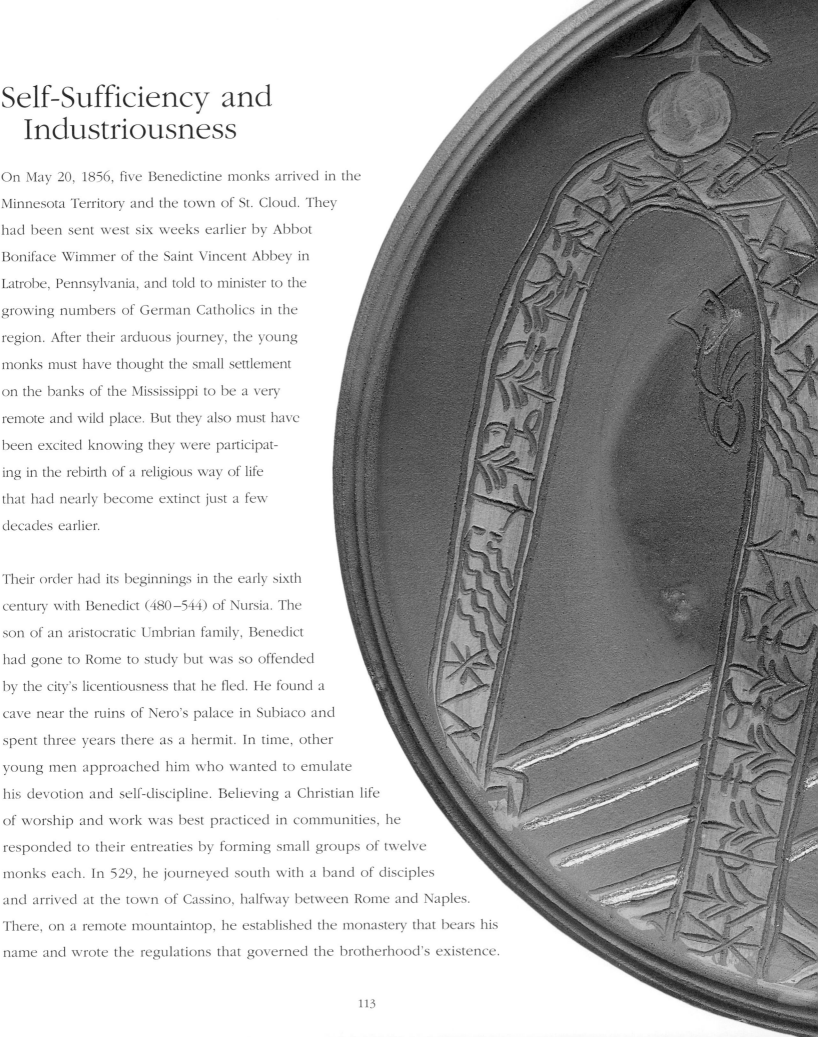

Benedict's "Rule," as it became known, was unusual in stressing moderation over austerity, order over arbitrariness. The Benedictine novice promised "stability, fidelity to monastic life, and obedience" (*Rule*, 58) and in so doing, bound himself to the monastic community for life. In turn, the monks selected a spiritual leader from their own ranks—an abbot who would also serve until his death. The abbot, writes Benedict, ought "rather to be of help than to command." He should "let mercy triumph over judgment . . . and strive to be loved rather than feared" (*Rule*, 64). Most importantly, the abbot should consult with all the monks, even the youngest, on matters of importance and carefully consider their opinions before making a final decision. "Do everything with counsel," says Benedict, "and you will not be sorry afterward" (*Rule*, 3). Moreover, while the abbot had to lead by example and enforce discipline, he was instructed not to "overdrive" his monks or give them cause for "just murmuring."

Benedict also prescribed the monks' routine behavior. Since his was a "school for the service of the Lord," the most important duty of all was worship, with the Divine Office being prayed seven times a day. The rule of silence was to be observed during meals, with one monk reading aloud from the Scriptures and other edifying materials. Four hours daily were to be spent alone, studying and meditating. And finally, to provide for their own needs, the monks had to do manual labor, especially fieldwork, six hours every day.

Teapot (Johanna kiln, Tanegashima chamber), 1995, stoneware, 6 in. high. Reed handle by Paul Krueger. To prevent unglazed wares from fusing together during the firing, Bresnahan uses wild rice hulls as a buffering agent. The hulls have an added benefit: they react with the intense heat of the kiln, giving the dark clay a rich metallic luster. Photograph by Gary Mortensen.

Covered bowl and cup (Johanna kiln, Tanegashima chamber), 1995, stoneware, 5 in. high (bowl with lid), 3½ in. high (cup). Reed handle by Paul Krueger. Because Bresnahan uses the intense flames of the firing to help create surface effects on his pots, he gives careful consideration to how he loads them in the kiln. By inverting this bowl over the cup and then placing the lid over the bowl's foot (as pictured), he ensured a wide range of colors and subtle textures on the pieces. Photograph by Gary Mortensen.

Melon-shaped spice jar (Johanna kiln, front fire chamber), 1997, stoneware with natural ash glaze, 4¹/₂ in. high.
Photograph by Gary Mortensen.

who became Bishop of Rome in 590 and the last of the four doctors of the Latin church. In fact, over their 1,500-year history, the Benedictines have had fifty monks elected to the papacy, as well as scores of cardinals, archbishops, and bishops.

But during the wave of secularism that swept Europe after the Napoleonic Wars, monastic lands and possessions were confiscated and Benedictine monks forced to leave their secluded enclaves. By 1814, only thirty monasteries remained from the hundreds that had originally existed on the Continent. Maximilian I of Bavaria even seized the great Abbey of Metten, which had been founded by Charlemagne in 792, and cast out its monks. Fortunately, Ludwig I reversed Maximilian's ecclesiastical policies, raised the necessary funds to buy the monastery himself, and then gave it back to the Catholic Church. In 1830, the last two surviving monks of Metten returned and began accepting novices a few years later. Among their recruits was Boniface Wimmer, who crossed the

Eventually, not only did most European monasteries adopt a similar code of conduct, but the Benedictines themselves nurtured some of the most vigorous leaders of Christianity, starting with Saint Gregory,

Five-footed bowls (Johanna kiln, Tanegashima chamber), 1999, stoneware, 3 in. high (each).
Photograph by Gary Mortensen.

Atlantic in 1846 to establish the first Benedictine monastery in America in Pennsylvania. And ten years later, it was he who, in turn, sent his own small delegation of monks westward to help settle the St. Cloud area (Barry, *Worship and Work*, pp. 6–25).

Soon after their arrival, the young Benedictines began celebrating Mass and the Divine Office in a makeshift chapel on the banks of the Mississippi. A year later, they admitted their first five students to their fledgling seminary and college. Over time, others joined them,

Small bottle (Johanna kiln, front fire chamber), 1995, stoneware with natural ash glaze, 7 1/8 in. high. As part of his commitment to making vessels for daily use, Bresnahan routinely produces small serving bottles. Inspired by the flasks the Japanese use for sake (rice wine), he created these pieces with long necks for easy pouring and broad flat bases for stability. One side of this bottle, which was directly hit by the intense heat of the firing, turned a matte yellow, while the portion facing away from the flames became a lustrous brown.
Photograph by Gary Mortensen.

and they moved their base of operation several times. But in 1866, they began to build a permanent monastery in an area known as "Indianbush." Four miles west of St. Cloud, the parcel of land had once been home to the Sioux and Chippewa. Under U.S. law, settlers could lay claim to the unoccupied territory. By combining their legal allotments, eight Benedictines eventually staked out 2,500 acres, which included pastureland, forests, and lakes (Barry, p. 44). The

Bottles with three lugs (Johanna kiln, front fire chamber), 1997, stoneware with natural ash glaze, 14 1/8 in. high, 15 1/2 in. high, 14 3/4 in. high (left to right). Bresnahan suspended these bottles horizontally in the front fire chamber of the kiln, supporting them at their feet and mouths. The natural ash glaze that accumulated on the upward-facing sides eventually dripped down, encircling the vessels with the dynamic tendril patterns seen here. Photograph by Gary Mortensen.

Plowed-field bowl (Johanna kiln, glaze chamber), 1997, stoneware with navy-bean straw ash glaze, 12 1/8 in. diameter.
Photograph by Gary Mortensen.

largest of these spring-fed bodies of water was called Lake Sagatagan, after its original Indian name.

Almost immediately, the monks also started constructing their first building—a multipurpose structure made from fieldstones they gathered from the nearby hillsides. Even before beginning the "Old Stone House," however, they had asked Abbot Boniface Wimmer to petition Rome, requesting that their monastery be elevated to abbey status. And by year's end, they had elected Rupert Seidenbusch, who had been the prior at Saint Vincent's in Pennsylvania, to be their first abbot (Barry, pp. 83–84, 95).

Under Abbot Rupert's tenure (1866–75) and the leaderships of his able successors—Alexius Edelbrock (1875–89), Bernard Locnikar (1890–94), and Peter Engel (1894–1921)—the early generations of monks at Saint John's created a community based on their fierce determination to succeed and their own innate resourcefulness. After finishing the "Old Stone House," they built kilns and fired their own bricks from clay deposits they found on site. For their first abbey church, which was begun in 1879, they operated their brickyard around-the-clock for months on end and produced 15,000 bricks a day (Barry, pp. 141–42). In addition to skilled masons and bricklayers, the monks also had talented carpenters among their numbers. After damming Watab Creek and erecting their own waterpowered sawmill, they cut down their own trees, milled their own lumber, helped erect the monastery's new buildings, and crafted sturdy furniture and other utilitarian objects.

On the monastery's vast acreage, the monks also grew wheat and rye, which they ground at their own gristmill and baked into large loaves of dark and hearty "Johnnie bread." They planted a sizable orchard and pressed their own cider and made apple butter. They even established a vineyard so they could harvest their own grapes for wine. In summer, they tended vast vegetable gardens and canned their own produce. They kept honeybees, both for the honey and the wax, and tapped hundreds of maple trees in the spring for the sap, which they boiled down for syrup and sugar. They not only raised chickens and pigs, but dairy cattle, whose milk they pasteurized for drinking and also processed for butter and cheese.

Tea bowl **(Johanna kiln, glaze chamber), 1995, stoneware with navy-bean straw ash glaze, 2 3/8 in. high, 5 1/8 in. diameter.**
Photograph by Gary Mortensen.

In all of these undertakings, the monks lived in accordance with one of Benedict's primary beliefs, as reflected in the motto *ora et labora*, worship and work. From the beginning, Benedict had always stressed the importance of self-sufficiency and the necessity of work, saying "Idleness is the enemy of the soul" (*Rule*, 48). And while physical labor proved essential during the early decades of the monastery and school for their very existence, the desire to engage in some kind of physical activity continues to this day. Saint John's current university president, Brother Dietrich Reinhart, explains that this idea is implicit in the Latin phrase *utilis occupatio*, "useful work," or "useful occupation." "A good monk," he says, "should also have a little garden plot or play an instrument—something to keep the whole of his life from becoming only cerebral and contemplative."

On October 3, 1979, Abbot Jerome Theisen blessed Bresnahan's first wood-burning kiln at Saint John's, which Bresnahan had named Takigama after his Japanese teacher's first son. Believing in the Benedictine philoso-phy of *ora et labora* (worship and work), Abbot Jerome assigned five novices to help build the kiln as part of their daily afternoon labor.
Photograph by Richard Bresnahan, 1979.

In encouraging Bresnahan to return to Saint John's during the late 1970s, Father Michael Blecker also might have been attempting to revive the monastery's hand-wrought traditions, which had somewhat subsided over the years. The flourmill had been shut down during the mid-1940s, the dairy closed in 1958, and the orchard and gardens scaled back from what they once were. By the time Father Michael became president in 1971, many of the "useful occupations" from earlier years had been abandoned as Saint John's modernized and more cost-effective alternatives became available. In Bresnahan, he saw a devotion to physical industriousness that had characterized Saint John's since its founding. Perhaps he also hoped the tenacious young potter would serve as a good example to the novices. Abbot Jerome Theisen must have certainly thought so when he sent five of them to help Bresnahan construct his first kiln in 1979.

At the same time, Father Michael was deeply aware of the high value Benedictines have always placed on the communal goods of the monastery, which strictly forbids private ownership. In describing the position of "cellarer," or keeper of the monastery's belongings, Benedict writes, "He will regard all utensils and goods of the monastery as sacred vessels of the altar, aware that nothing is to be neglected" (*Rule*, 31). While this respect for things encompasses all goods, regardless of whether they are made inside the monastery or out, it seems likely that Father Michael felt some nostalgia for a time when nearly everything used by the monks was either created by them or others who lived on the grounds.

That Bresnahan was committed to producing hand-crafted objects that not only were functional but made from local materials could only reinforce this Benedictine ideal. Brother Dennis Beach, who currently teaches philosophy at Saint John's, perhaps said it best when he observed, "There is an everyday quality to monastic life, and that is another reason why a potter made sense. And there is something about clay, its very ordinariness, and finding the sacred within it that is very Benedictine in character."

Tea bowl (Johanna kiln, glaze chamber), 1995, stoneware with navy-bean straw ash glaze, 2 3/4 in. high, 5 1/8 in. diameter.
Photograph by Gary Mortensen.

Situated on 2,500 acres of lakes, forests, and grasslands in central Minnesota, Saint John's Abbey and University were built on land the founding monks called *Schoenthal* (beautiful valley). This aerial view shows the campus as it appears today. The main thoroughfare leads to Marcel Breuer's 1961 sculptural bell banner and abbey church. The red brick buildings next to the church date to the 19th century and were constructed by the monks themselves from bricks they had made and fired in their own kilns. At the upper right, smoke can be seen rising from the chimney of the Johanna kiln.

Photograph by Steven Bergerson, October 1998.

A Place of Great Beauty—
Holy Before We Arrived

The careful frugality and deep-seated pragmatism of the Benedictines in no way lessen their appreciation of art and beauty. In fact, it was the physical splendor of the "Indianbush" itself that had prompted Saint John's first monks to lay claim to it initially. While a few of their group had wanted to establish the monastery in St. Cloud, Father Bruno Riess insisted that the untamed wilderness of the Indianbush held far greater promise. With permission from his prior, he spent one day a week exploring it, and it was he who escorted Abbot Boniface Wimmer to the area in 1856. Later, when the monks began building their "claim" cabins, they dubbed the northern Watab basin *Schoenthal*, or "beautiful valley" (Barry, *Worship and Work*, pp. 44–45). Even in the 1990s, when complimented about Saint John's natural majesty, Abbot Timothy Kelly said—partly because of Benedictine modesty but mostly because it was true—"This has always been a place of great beauty—a place holy before we arrived."

Undoubtedly, Father Michael Blecker's admiration for Bresnahan and his pottery stemmed from his own appreciation of art and the Benedictine reverence for the aesthetically pleasing. "Within monastic life," says Brother Dietrich Reinhart, "there is a high value placed on the material

Landscape vase (Johanna kiln, front fire chamber), 1995, stoneware with slip painting and natural ash glaze, 14 in. high. Bresnahan painted this vessel with diagonal sweeps of the brush to suggest windblown rain hitting plowed farmland. The sprinkling of ash glaze and dramatic color variations that occurred during the firing contribute to the impression of a violent storm.
Photograph by Gary Mortensen.

Completed in 1880, Saint John's original abbey church was an impressive Romanesque structure with two 150-foot towers. A few years later, the monks added three adjoining buildings, forming a quadrangle with an interior courtyard.
Late 19th century.

The interior of Saint John's original abbey church showing the blessing of Abbot Baldwin Dworschak and the paintings of Brother Clement Frischauf.
Photograph by John L. Loveland, 1951.

Brother Clement Frischauf painted in a style originally developed by the monks of Beuron Abbey in southern Germany. His decorations for the interior of Saint John's original abbey church are the most significant examples of Beuronese art in America.
Early 1940s.

world and the creative process. There is also an ongoing debate about what art is and what is the most respectable way to adorn churches and create spaces that nurture a community and lead to something far grander and more ennobling."

Boniface Wimmer, America's first Benedictine abbot, also had recognized the significance of art in cultivating the soul. In a letter to Ludwig I of Bavaria in 1849, he wrote: "I am determined to have our monasteries not only schools of religion and of the sciences, but also nurseries of the fine arts," for "I am fully convinced that a monastic school which does not promote the . . . fine arts . . . is very incomplete" (Barry, p. 335).

Consequently, not only did Saint John's earliest students receive instruction in the arts but the monks who founded the monastery brought handcrafted objects with them from Europe to aid in the process. In the few wooden crates they transported they had "three missals, a fine ostensorium, ciborium, three chalices, and breviaries for the *Opus Dei*" (Barry, p. 23). Not only were these objects of vital importance to their religious and educational mission, they were a tangible link to Europe's great artistic heritage. "The constant attention given to altar vessels, church decoration and furniture, bells and organs," writes Father Colman Barry, was "an exterior expression of the traditional customs these Catholic people were in the process of transplanting from Europe to America" (Barry, p. 89).

In designing Saint John's original abbey church in 1879, Father Gregory Steil also looked to European

examples and created an impressive Romanesque structure with two 150-foot towers. Even the massive marble altar he devised had an architecturally inspired Romanesque baldachin. A few years later, he added three five-storied buildings to the church to form a quadrangle. This arrangement, typical of many European monasteries, enclosed a central courtyard laid out with trees and flower gardens. The additions gave the complex an imposing appearance similar to that of Metten Abbey—Saint John's own "mother" institution in Bavaria on the Danube.

In the 1930s, Saint John's invited Brother Clement Frischauf to adorn the abbey's refectory with wall murals. A student of Desiderius Lenz, Brother Clement was one of the founders of the Beuronese style, which drew inspiration from the geometrical simplifications of Egyptian, Greek, and early Christian art. Brother Clement had already undertaken several major commissions in Europe, including working with Lenz at Monte Cassino for fourteen years on various paintings and mosaics. He eventually joined Saint John's community and took on the ambitious project of decorating the interior of the abbey church itself. His paintings there remain the most significant and extensive examples of Beuronese art in the United States (Hauser, *Sacred Art*, pp. 34–37).

But nowhere is Saint John's commitment to the arts more clearly demonstrated than in its 1953 decision to ask architect Marcel Breuer to develop a comprehensive building program for them. Trained at the Bauhaus in the 1920s, Breuer, a Hungarian Jew, left Germany in 1935, immigrating first to

In 1953, the monks of Saint John's commissioned Hungarian architect Marcel Breuer to develop a comprehensive building program for them. Ten of Breuer's designs have been constructed, including this famous church with its monumental bell banner.
Photograph by Lee Hanley, 1961.

Designed by Marcel Breuer, the Alcuin Memorial Library at Saint John's features two gigantic tree forms that support the weight of the roof and are made from reinforced concrete.
Photograph by Bill Hedrich, 1964.

England and then the United States. Although he had already collaborated on the design of the UNESCO Building in Paris, Breuer had not been given any major American commissions until he received Saint John's offer. Breuer's "100 Year Plan" for both the university and monastery did not disappoint. It not only addressed the need for expansion but reflected modern ideals, which emphasized the philosophy of form following function and the use of such 20th-century materials as steel and ferroconcrete (concrete reinforced with steel bars or mesh).

All told, Saint John's built ten of Breuer's designs, including a new abbey church (1958–61), a monastic wing (1955), two libraries (1964, 1975), a science hall (1968), an ecumenical center (1968), and four dormitories (1959, 1967). Of these, the abbey church, with its colossal bell tower, takes center stage as *the* jewel in the crown. Like a gigantic abstract sculpture, the 112-foot-high bell tower, or "banner" as Breuer called it, stands at the front of the building. A concrete gateway to the church, it has two rectangular openings at its

upper reaches: the higher one holds a white oak cross fabricated in Saint John's own carpentry shop, and the lower opening contains five bronze bells to call the faithful to worship.

The church itself is an immense rhomboid, its soaring height supported by eleven massive concrete "folds" rather than columns. Centrally located, the altar dominates the interior, with choir stalls radiating in

Canisters (Johanna kiln, Tanegashima chamber), 1995, stoneware, 12 1/2 in. high (each). Bresnahan used the same clay for these canisters and fired them both in the third, or Tanegashima, chamber of the Johanna kiln. But each vessel has a very different surface, which was caused by the way the kiln's intense heat caressed it. In some areas, the clay flashed a brilliant red. Elsewhere, the heat reacted with wild rice hulls to create swirling iridescent patterns.

Photograph by Gary Mortensen.

Iris platter (Johanna kiln, glaze chamber), 1995, stoneware with iron and white slip painting under an elm ash glaze, 14 1/2 in. diameter.

Photograph by Gary Mortensen.

Spiral cups (Johanna kiln, front fire chamber), 1995, stoneware with slip painting and natural ash glaze, 5 1/2 in. high (each).

Photograph by Gary Mortensen.

During his apprenticeship in Karatsu, Bresnahan saw how the Japanese hearth (*irori*) brought family and guests together several times a day to share tea, food, and warmth. When he returned to Saint John's, he also witnessed the importance of ritual in Benedictine life. These observances caused him to make daily routines part of his own existence as well. He built an *irori* in his studio so he could meet regularly with his apprentices over a cup of tea and often invites people visiting the pottery to join them.

Photograph of Nakazato Takashi's *irori* by Richard Bresnahan, 1978.
Photograph of Saint John's 1961 abbey church by Brother Robin Pierzina, 1981.

a semicircle around it and opening out onto the pews. Considered to be one of the most splendid churches in America, the sanctuary glows with a honeycomb of light, which comes through 564 stained-glass windows designed by Bronislaw Bak and made by Saint John's own monks and students. The altar is lit from above by a modern stained-glass lantern in rich yellows and oranges by the famous Bauhaus designer Josef Albers.

With the construction of Breuer's abbey church completed, Saint John's redoubled its efforts to collect sacred art. A powerful bronze sculpture by Doris Caesar of Saint John the Baptist—the monastery's patron saint—now stands in the abbey's baptistry. Works by such eminent American and European artists as Leonard Baskin, Joseph O'Connell, Gerhardt Marcks, Jean Lambert-Rucki, Mark Macken, Peter Watts, and Meinrad Burch also have been purchased to adorn the thirty-four private chapels inside the church's crypt. In addition, Josef Albers designed a window for the abbot's chapel, and Breuer himself contributed a monumental sculpture of two interlocking forms called "Wrestlers" for the front lawn of the athletic complex.

Moreover, Saint John's visionary approach to the arts continues. In 1998, the monastery commissioned Donald Jackson, scribe to England's House of Lords and Queen Elizabeth II, to oversee the production of the first handwritten and illuminated Bible to be created in the past five hundred years. The seven-volume work will take more than six years to complete and involve the efforts of four skilled calligraphers. Most recently, after reviewing fifty prestigious architectural firms, Saint John's selected Japanese architect Andō Tadao to design a new guest house for the monastery.

Just as importantly, Saint John's has had a long tradition of artists in its own ranks, including Brother Placid Stuckenschneider. A graphic artist of considerable talent, Brother Placid drew illustrations and designs for the Liturgical Press, the abbey's publishing house. After studying silversmithing with Father Ignatius Wiltzius, Father Baldwin Dworschak cast a chalice for his own ordination into the priesthood in 1933. For the past fifty years, Claustral Oblate Frank Kacmarcik, who taught art history and studio classes at Saint John's, has designed the covers of *Worship*, the Liturgical Press's bimonthly journal, and in 1995, he donated his extensive collection of books, prints, and drawings to the university. Father Hugh Witzmann taught sculpture between 1960 and 1997 and has created and exhibited

Large jar (Johanna kiln, front fire chamber), 1995, stoneware with paddled decor and natural ash glaze, 24 in. high. To make a large jar, Bresnahan begins with a flattened slab of clay for the base. Using clay coils, he then slowly builds up the vessel's sides. He twists each coil, pressing and pinching it to the previous one. He then gently beats the jar's exterior with a carved wooden paddle, compressing the clay for greater strength and creating shallow patterns on the surface. This process often results in slightly irregular forms. Far from being a drawback, such imperfections enhance the unique character of each piece.
Photograph by Gary Mortensen.

many of his pieces on campus and at the monastery. For the last twenty-five years, Father Jerome Tupa, who teaches French, also has painted numerous abstract and representational images with spiritual themes. An artist with an international reputation, Father Jerome maintains a humble studio above the woodworking shop at Saint John's and has gallery representation in Los Angeles and Scottsdale, Arizona.

Within this environment of valuing art and artists, Father Michael Blecker's support of Richard Bresnahan seems natural, for he must have seen the young potter as part of an ongoing tradition of creativity that has enhanced life at Saint John's since the beginning. And while Bresnahan's art was rarely liturgical, it did reflect Saint John's in a unique way. By using local materials for his works and fueling his kiln with deadfall from the surrounding forests, Bresnahan creates pieces that mirror Saint John's very essence—both its body and its soul. In fact, Bresnahan's handmade pottery has become so entwined with Saint John's identity that his works are routinely given to important guests who visit the monastery and taken to faraway places and offered as gifts.

Since the monastery's founding in the mid-1850s, the monks of Saint John's Abbey have always had skilled craftsmen and artists among their ranks. Father Jerome Tupa, who has taught French at the university since 1976, also maintains a painting studio on campus.
Photograph by James R. Dean, 2000.

The monks of Saint John's Abbey have always milled their own lumber and crafted sturdy wooden furniture and other utilitarian objects. Brother Hubert Schneider ran the woodworking shop for 56 years until he retired in 1991. Even then, he continued to sharpen the shop's various saws and planes every Saturday morning.
Photograph by Brother Robin Pierzina, 1987.

The monks of Saint John's celebrated the blessing of Abbot John Klassen in December 2000. In the Benedictine tradition, Abbot John strongly advocates greater sensitivity to the natural environment and its preservation.
Photograph by Greg Becker, 2001.

Stewards of the Earth

When Father Michael Blecker invited Bresnahan to set up a pottery at Saint John's, he already knew a great deal about the young artist's experience in Japan from letters Bresnahan had sent back to his academic advisors. He also was keenly aware of Bresnahan's ambitious desire to establish a pottery with a regional style. But as Bresnahan toiled through the summer and fall of 1979, something else became clear to him and the other monks at Saint John's. For by salvaging industrial wastes, firing with deadfall, and using other natural resources in a responsible way, Bresnahan was conducting himself in a very Benedictine manner.

The current abbot of Saint John's, John Klassen, lists the three recurring themes in Benedict's *Rule* that underscore the importance of environmental stewardship—humility, stability, and frugality. Humility allows Benedictines to recognize that humans are only part of a larger whole, he explains, and thus gives them respect for other creatures and the natural world. Stability involves a life-long commitment to a certain place and a community. "By coming to know a place deeply," he writes, and "the delicate balance" that

exists between its inhabitants and the natural environment, as well as "the patterns that play themselves out year after year," enables "monastic communities to make decisions with an understanding of their consequences." And by practicing frugality, monks can evaluate their true needs in light of mere desires, helping them to avoid rampant consumerism (Klassen, "The Rule of Benedict and Environmental Stewardship," 1998).

These Benedictine virtues permeate nearly every aspect of monastic life at Saint John's and its ongoing commitment to environmentalism. The lumber shed behind the woodworking shop on campus, for example, houses an astonishing array of cast-off furniture and architectural fragments, as well as numerous bins of curing lumber.

Canister (Johanna kiln, glaze chamber), 2000, stoneware with oak ash glaze, 14 1/4 in. high.
Photograph by Gary Mortensen.

Double-gourd teapot (Johanna kiln, front fire chamber), 1999, stoneware with iron slip painting and natural ash glaze, 7 in. high. Reed handle by Paul Krueger.
Photograph by Gary Mortensen.

Tea bowl (Johanna kiln, glaze chamber), 1995, stoneware with sunflower-seed hull ash glaze, 2 5/8 in. high, 5 1/4 in. diameter. Sixteenth-century Japanese tea masters popularized the use of low cylindrical tea bowls. The generous proportions and open mouth of this tea bowl complement the complex golden tonalities of its glaze, which was produced from sunflower-seed hull ash. Committed to using local resources, Bresnahan depends on waste ash from Cargill's Multi-Seed Processing and Refining Plant in West Fargo, North Dakota, for the glaze's primary ingredient.
Photograph by Gary Mortensen.

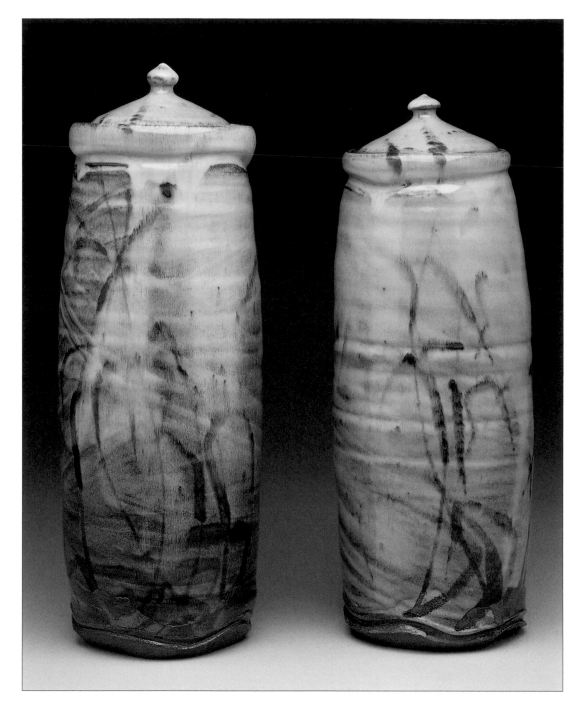

Canisters (Johanna kiln, glaze chamber), 1998, stoneware with white slip and iron painting under a navy-bean straw ash glaze, 14 1/2 in. high (left), 13 5/8 in. high (right). Inspired by painted Karatsu ware, Bresnahan decorates his vessels with images from his own natural surroundings in the Midwest. The simple compositions here feature stalks of wheat.
Photograph by Gary Mortensen.

Throughout Saint John's history, the monks have had an active role in making and furnishing the monastery's and school's various buildings. This has been true even when the scale of a project necessitated employing outside construction firms and carpenters. Over time, as some structures have been remodeled and others demolished, parts of them have always been salvaged and stored in the lumber shed until they can be refurbished and put to a new use. In fact, Father Alfred Deutsch wrote admiringly about his fellow monk Brother Hubert Schneider. Brother Hubert ran the woodworking shop for decades, and Father Alfred likened him to an archivist or curator, preserving the monastery's history by knowing "where and how this bundle of molding, that wainscoting, or those chairs had once been used" (Deutsch, "The Carpenter Shop," pp. 31–38).

It comes as no surprise, then, that when Bresnahan was constructing his first kiln on campus, he found some of the bricks he needed in Saint John's very own stockpiles of used materials. Watching Bresnahan build his kiln from salvaged incinerator bricks must have caused Father Michael Blecker and the other monks to sense that they had found a kindred spirit in the frugal young potter. And seeing this again and again as Bresnahan put discarded materials to good use only could have deepened their respect for him and eventual acceptance into their world.

This Benedictine notion of stewardship extends beyond the built environment to the natural one. Through responsible harvesting and replanting of trees, the monastery has not only preserved the beauty of its natural setting but ensured a reliable source for lumber. When Father Paul Schweitz, the first director of Saint John's arboretum, visited ancient Benedictine monasteries in Europe, he was humbled to discover that they all had long histories of land management, some with one hundred- to 150-year rotation cycles for their trees. They construct buildings, make furniture, and fuel boilers from the lumber they harvest, he explained, just as the monks of Saint John's have been doing since they first entered the Indianbush. "But what I especially realized during my trip," he said, was "that Benedictines are not afraid to use resources, but do so in a responsible way. And that's a hallmark of Benedictine principles about stewardship—it is not a hands-off policy."

By producing functional wares and firing them from a renewable resource, Bresnahan practices a similar philosophy. Likewise, the filtration system he installed at his studio to reclaim the water used for washing clay also demonstrates a concern for the future. Even Bresnahan's stockpile of 18,000 tons of clay guarantees that the pottery will be sustainable well beyond his own lifetime. "The Native Americans say 'to the seventh generation,'" states Father Paul. "But we don't limit it to that generation, and that's really the Benedictine ideal."

Pitcher (Johanna kiln, glaze chamber), 1995, stoneware with navy-bean straw ash glaze, 11 in. high.
Photograph by Gary Mortensen.

Renewal

During his first decade at Saint John's, Bresnahan had been remarkably successful. He had transformed an abandoned root cellar into a vital pottery. His strong work ethic accorded well with Benedictine beliefs, as did his determination to operate his studio in an environmentally responsible way with sustainable local resources. Through his many accomplishments, he had garnered financial support from local foundations and had cultivated a considerable following among the faculty, students, and nearby communities. Despite this, his future at Saint John's remained tenuous.

For many years, the university's regents had recognized the need for a more centrally located student union. Starting with their earliest conversations, they had agreed to raze humble "Joe" Hall and its unattractive garage to make way for the new facility. But because of a lack of funds, the project had languished. During the late 1980s, however, the university embarked on a capital campaign, and in 1991, when Brother Dietrich Reinhart took office as president, the student center suddenly became the focus for the school's fund-raising efforts.

Opposite page: Bresnahan with his mentor, Sister Johanna Becker.
Photograph by Annette Brophy, 1997.

"I was faced with tearing down Joe Hall and the choice of either getting rid of Richard or finding money to put him in a new space," Brother Dietrich says. "And it wasn't in anybody's financial planning. It wasn't in the board's fund-raising strategy, and there was no space on campus where Richard could go that people could agree on." Compounding his dilemma was the fact that enrollment projections for the 1991–92 academic year had come up short, resulting in a million dollar deficit.

Serving plate (Johanna kiln, Tanegashima chamber), 2000, stoneware with natural ash glaze, 10 ¼ in. diameter.
Photograph by Gary Mortensen.

Teapot (Johanna kiln, Tanegashima chamber), 2000, stoneware, 9 ⅛ in. high. When his longtime friend and collaborator Paul Krueger became ill and was unable to weave reed handles for his teapots, Bresnahan began to experiment with making ceramic ones. Unlike the delicate appendages seen on many porcelain pots, Bresnahan's handles are both functional and sturdy. For this vessel, he designed a muscular grip and spout. To keep the overall form from seeming too ponderous, he elongated its body and shaped the base with a flaring skirt, which hides an unusual inset foot.
Photograph by Gary Mortensen.

In despair, Brother Dietrich turned to Brother Linus Ascheman, a classmate who had joined the monastery at the same time he had. Like Brother Dietrich, Brother Linus, who was director of buildings and grounds, was new at his position. As his friend described his predicament, Brother Linus suggested that Joe Hall be moved instead of torn down. "Oh sure," responded Brother Dietrich in disbelief, "and let's build a tree house while we're at it." But Brother Linus remained steadfast in his thinking. Joe Hall was a substantial brick building, he reasoned, but not so large to preclude it from being relocated. Given the function of the pottery, it could be on the west side of campus, next to the art building and near the woodworking shop and power plant. But no open area there existed. Then Brother Linus offered another solution: they could create space for it by moving the Seidenbush Apartments to the north side of campus, where all the other dormitories were situated. It was a complex plan and involved moving not only one building but two. Still, Brother Dietrich felt a glimmer of hope.

Excited by the possibility, the two took their clipboards and strolled out into the night. A few minutes later, they were standing inside Joe Hall, rapping on doors in the hallway. The students thought it was a raid—a late night check for alcohol or some other mischief by the new president himself. But on the contrary, Brother Dietrich and Brother Linus were shining their flashlights up and down the walls and across the ceilings, assessing whether the building was in good enough condition to warrant saving.

By voting to save "Joe" Hall, the monks of Saint John's demonstrated their belief in historic preservation. Their decision also revealed the high value Benedictines place on reusing materials rather than discarding them. Here, the 780-ton building is being prepared for the move to its new location on campus.
Photograph by Paul A. Wegner, Summer 1992.

Later that month, Brother Dietrich met with Frank Ladner, one of the university's regents, to prepare for a finance committee meeting. The issue of the pottery was not on the next day's agenda, but Brother Dietrich needed to confide in someone. So he outlined the pottery's history to Ladner and explained the complicated idea for moving Joe Hall. He admitted he did not know how the project would be financed and conceded that internal opposition would probably arise, especially from the university's comptroller, Father Gordon Tavis. Nonetheless, Brother Dietrich said, Bresnahan and the pottery were important to Saint John's, and maybe the finance committee could at least discuss the subject at their winter gathering, in three months' time.

The very next day, however, Ladner suddenly announced to the finance committee that "Brother Dietrich has an idea he would like to share with you about the pottery." Unprepared and somewhat taken aback, the young president tentatively launched into a description of the complex scheme. Tense and emotionally exhausted, he was suddenly overwhelmed by the specter of losing the pottery—and Joe Hall— and started to cry, all the while still explaining his seemingly implausible plan to the astonished group. After Brother Dietrich had finished, Father Gordon was the first to speak. "I think it is a brilliant idea," he said, wiping tears from his own eyes. Brother Dietrich was astounded. The internal politics of the committee had shifted, and all at once they were discussing ways to make the plan feasible.

After first being introduced to Bresnahan in Japan in 1976, Mary Burke, an internationally renowned collector of Japanese art, visited him at his Saint John's studio in 1996. Here, she (right) meets with author Matthew Welch (left), Sister Colman O'Connell of the College of Saint Benedict, and Brother Dietrich Reinhart of Saint John's University.
Photograph by James R. Dean, 1996.

Vase **(Johanna kiln, glaze chamber), 1995, stoneware with navy-bean straw ash glaze, 13 1/2 in. high.**
Photograph by Gary Mortensen.

To relocate the 780-ton brick structure, a team of professionals first lifted it on pneumatic jacks and then built a steel framework underneath it that rested on 216 airplane wheels. Using railroad ties, they also laid a temporary roadway to the new site. To lessen damage to the building, they moved it with extreme slowness, sometimes no more than ten feet a day.

Photograph by Paul A. Wegner, Summer 1992.

While the finance committee proved to be a significant ally for saving the pottery, the battle was far from over. Brother Dietrich still had to win approval from the monastery's chapter, the assembly of all the monks who belong to Saint John's, and he soon found himself standing in judgment before them, pleading his case. By moving Joe Hall, he explained, they could preserve a historic building—part of Saint John's own illustrious past. They could recoup the cost of relocating it—and constructing a new basement to house the pottery—by continuing to use the upper floors of the structure as dormitory rooms. But he also encouraged the monks to dream of a different function for those two stories. Since the building was to be situated on the "industrial"

side of campus, he said, perhaps it could serve not only as a studio for the pottery but for the monastery's own artists as well. The idea hit a responsive cord, and by the end of the discussion, the plan seemed so reasonable that an overwhelming majority voted for it. "By the time it was all over," he recounts, "a couple of monks came over to me and said, 'Dietrich, you could sell refrigerators to Eskimos.'"

Ultimately, Joe Hall's relocation, coupled with the pottery's rejuvenation, captured everyone's imagination. In the summer of 1992, a team of professional building movers from Long Lake, Minnesota, slowly lifted the 780-ton building on pneumatic jacks. Then beneath it, they fabricated a steel framework that rested on 216 airplane wheels made for Boeing 747s. Kept level by the same hydraulic system jets use, the structure finally was ready to be moved. To the lively tunes of a marching band, the building slowly began its five-hundred-yard journey, pulled by a single truck. At the sight of it, Brother Dietrich experienced a sudden pang of apprehension. "It had to go down a hill," he said, "and at the bottom of that hill is a lake. And I thought, 'This could be the shortest Saint John's presidency on record.'" But six weeks later, amid great fanfare and a collective sigh of relief, the building was safely lowered onto its new stone foundation.

It has been nearly a decade since Brother Dietrich Reinhart argued to save Joe Hall and thus renew the university's commitment to Richard Bresnahan and his pottery. But to this day, his belief in the studio's significance to Saint John's remains unshakable. "The pottery anchors the university in a rich heritage of craftsmanship and artistry," he says. "That is an important ingredient in a grounded life and in binding communities together. It is also a vital component of a liberal arts education. The pottery connects people to Saint John's who would have no other connection to us. It is a resource in the area, and in that sense, it calls to mind the great medieval monasteries of Europe that became centers of learning, stability, and influence."

"Joe" Hall in its present location on the west side of campus. Sculptor Tadd Jensen sheathed the building's new foundation with local fieldstone. The entrance to Bresnahan's studio, which occupies the lower level, is shown here.
Photograph by James R. Dean, 1993.

An Unlikely Teacher

The Apprentices

When he returned from Japan in late 1978, Richard Bresnahan did not consider himself to be a teacher. He had declined two college positions because the issues he felt passionately about—local materials, wood firing, and sustainable resources—rarely were discussed in academic art programs with their conceptual approach to aesthetics. But after apprenticing with Nakazato Takashi, Bresnahan did believe in his own ability to be a working potter—to set up a studio, build a kiln, and produce functional wares.

John Sullivan (Grotto Foundation Apprentice, 2000), *Tea bowl*, 2000,
stoneware with natural ash glaze, 2 3/4 in. high, 5 3/8 in. diameter.
Photograph by Robert Fogt, 2001.

Opposite page: Jane Frees-Kluth (Jerome Foundation Emerging Artist, 1999), *Richard*, **1999, stoneware with natural ash glaze, 32 in. high. In creating a portrait of Bresnahan, Frees-Kluth wanted to convey how thoroughly he identifies with his craft. She convinced him to throw a medium-sized vase, which she altered into a torso form, using one of his carved paddles to texture the surface. She then joined a clay head of her own making to the bust, turning the vase's mouth into a turtlenecked sweater. Finally, she topped the head with a stack of Bresnahan's own pots. The overturned bowl recalls the cap he usually wears.**
Photograph by Robert Fogt, 2001.

Had he not broken his leg, he surely would have constructed his first wood-burning kiln in America largely by himself. But as it turned out, he needed to heavily depend on others during those first months at Saint John's. And when Thanos Johnson, a potter at a college in California, called to say that two of his students—Alan Peirson and Douglas Smith—would be willing apprentices, Bresnahan knew it was an offer he could not refuse. He could benefit from two full-time workers, and they, in turn, could profit by learning Japanese studio practices and potting techniques. And so, he agreed to take them on and in so doing reluctantly assumed the role of "master."

At about the same time Bresnahan was struggling to establish himself at Saint John's, Gerry Williams, a potter and the editor and cofounder of *Studio Potter*

Matthew Cartier (Grotto Foundation Apprentice, 1997–98), *Fat Monkey Jar,* **2000, stoneware with natural ash glaze, 6 in. high.**
Photograph by Robert Fogt, 2001.

journal, was compiling a book about the nature of apprenticeships. In his foreword, Williams describes apprenticing as part of America's rich craft traditions and especially valuable to those individuals who want to escape the impersonal approach of most large-scale programs. Despite its possible drawbacks, especially the legal ambiguities that exist between "apprentices" and "employees," the system proves vital in maintaining standards of craftsmanship during an era dominated by inferior, mass-produced goods.

Moreover, in accepting apprentices, the master also assumes the responsibility to not only impart technical training but to provide practical information about earning a living. "If the only purpose of the apprenticeship is to get the floor swept," Williams states, "it is dead before it starts. But if, instead, it can be seen as a living, growing relationship, with its own place in the creative environment, then it will have served its purpose" (Williams, *Apprenticeship in Craft*, p. 118).

While Williams attributed the reemergence of apprenticeships to the economic viability of craft as a livelihood, David A. Kolb explained the growing popularity of apprenticeships as a manifestation of how people best learn. In his 1984 study, Kolb argued that learning is essentially a social process that begins with a concrete experience followed by reflection, conceptualization, and experimentation. "Through experiences of imitation and communication with others and interaction with the physical environment," he writes, "internal developmental potentialities are enacted and practiced until they are internalized" (Kolb, *Experiential Learning*, p. 133).

Apprenticeships, as learning experiences that directly occur between masters and students, counter the depersonalization and conceptualization of modern society. "This learning process," Kolb states, "must be reimbued with the texture and feeling of human experiences shared and interpreted through dialogue with one another. In the overeager embrace of the rational, scientific, and technological, our concept of the learning process itself was distorted first by rationalism and later by behaviorism" (Kolb, p. 2).

While Bresnahan was not directly aware of these educational theories, he nonetheless practiced them by basing his own approach on his personal experiences, especially those gained from his master in Japan. The monks and teachers at Saint John's, however, were knowledgeable about experience-based learning as a method of instruction in colleges and universities. Not only had the concept been practiced there since its founding, but when Bresnahan arrived on campus in the late 1970s, master carpenters and bookbinders were still teaching apprentices their age-old crafts.

Jennifer Otis (Grotto Foundation Apprentice, 1999), *The Secret Life of Plants,* **1999, stoneware, 24 in. high. "I created works in this series as a tribute to the mystery, beauty, and medicinal power of plants. This piece was inspired by sumac leaves turning crimson in the fall. The natural ash deposits and color flashing from firing it also represent nature, but in a different way. For me, working with clay and wood firing are about honoring the cycles of nature."** Photograph by Robert Fogt, 2001.

Michael Carlson (Grotto Foundation Apprentice, 1999–2000), *Covered bowl, plate, and cup*, 2000, stoneware,
4 3/4 in. diameter, 8 in. diameter, 4 in. high (left to right).
Photograph by Robert Fogt, 2001.

Despite everyone's best intentions, Bresnahan had a somewhat frustrating time with his first two apprentices, as did they with him. Both students rose to the challenge of processing raw materials and building the Takigama kiln, which they helped fire twice. As they experimented with ways to outfit the fledgling studio with makeshift equipment, they also became skilled at improvisation. But while they each became proficient on the Karatsu-style kick wheel, they had next to no time to make their own pots, a situation that left them dispirited and resentful.

At the same time, Bresnahan could not offer them any monetary compensation because he had so little financial support himself. As their own bank accounts dwindled, both apprentices felt they needed to leave the studio to find better situations economically and did so within nine months.

Hoping to alleviate such hardships, Father Michael Blecker introduced Bresnahan to Aldred ("Al") Heckman, executive director of the Grotto Foundation, a charitable organization in St. Paul, Minnesota, that is committed to improving educational opportunities for people throughout the state. Previously, Heckman had agreed to fund the abbey's creation of a manuscript library, so he and the Grotto Foundation already had a strong relationship with Saint John's.

Heckman was so taken with Bresnahan's visionary approach and entrepreneurial spirit that he arranged for Louis W. Hill, Jr., who created the foundation, to visit the studio. Hill not only had a long history of subsidizing the arts but a keen interest in Japanese woodblock prints. With Hill's blessing, the studio began receiving annual grants from the Grotto Foundation in 1981, which help underwrite the apprentices' room and board at Saint John's. Since that time, twenty-four students have benefited from Grotto's support, with the average apprenticeship lasting a full year or more.

Like his Japanese master, Bresnahan has always demanded that his apprentices be totally committed to the studio. He expects them to keep long hours, six days a week, and requires that part of each day be spent on such mundane duties as cleaning the pottery and preparing clay and glazes.

"Kevin Flicker, Richard Bresnahan, and Kakutani Mitsuo have shown me how to use local materials and the benefits that come from a close relationship with your environment. I feel almost no attachment to pots that are made from clay I don't know or glazed with powder from a place I've never been." Michael Carlson (Grotto Foundation Apprentice, 1999–2000) and Bresnahan (left) glazing a large vase.
Photograph by James R. Dean, 1999.

Such tasks have always been part of a traditional Japanese system, writes John Singleton in his book about apprenticing in Japan, earning the student "the right to observe and learn by doing the menial scut work of the master and the workplace" (Singleton, *Learning in Likely Places*, p. 11).

While this autocratic approach runs counter to Bresnahan's democratic inclinations, he does think it is a necessary component of the apprenticeship, making each student thoroughly familiar with all aspects of running a studio. "Bresnahan often said that the more sensitive you become to the processes that go into the actual making of a pot," says former apprentice Stephen Earp, "be it digging your own clay, processing your

Stephen Earp (Grotto Foundation Apprentice, 1987–88), *Ring jug*, 2000, glazed redware with slip trailing, 11 ½ in. high. "I enjoy looking at early American (pre-1860) and English country pottery. I have been won over by their quiet, graceful lines. Those pots weren't trying to prove anything. They were simply made to be used. Within the redware tradition, I see the 'unassuming beauty' so often mentioned in discussions of Japanese folk ceramics. For this piece, I used humble redware because that is where the ring-jug form came from and making it again in my lifetime completes the circle."
Photograph by Robert Fogt, 2001.

"Working at Saint John's Pottery was one of those rare and special life-defining moments. The technical training I received, along with Bresnahan's practice of environmental conservation, continues to have an impact on the work I do. I wouldn't consider making my own pots without incorporating local materials in some way." Stephen Earp (Grotto Foundation Apprentice, 1987–88) throwing on a Karatsu-style kick wheel.
Photograph by James R. Dean, 1987.

own glaze materials, tending to the kiln instead of pushing buttons, working with a wheel rather than just throwing, or even recycling every little scrap of clay—the more it shows in your work." Bresnahan also believes that such regular activities as cleaning the studio, preparing tea, and wedging clay can become ritualistic actions that help center the potter and provide a consistent framework for the workday.

In addition, Bresnahan strongly adheres to the Japanese emphasis on *tsuchiaji*, or "clay taste." If a spiritual aspect to pottery exists, Bresnahan says, it is in the rediscovery of nature through the clay and its inherent qualities. This approach exalts the use of local materials and rejects the convenience of ordering preprocessed clays and glazes, which is standard practice in all university pottery programs.

Consequently, Bresnahan's apprentices must spend a substantial portion of their time preparing the studio's materials—digging raw clay out of his vast stockpile, bringing buckets of it to the pottery, washing out the impurities, and allowing the slurry to settle. Next, they must run it through the filter press, then the pug mill, and finally wedge it by hand until the clay possesses a fine, even consistency.

In remaining true to his Japanese training, Bresnahan also requires his apprentices to use the Karatsu-style kick wheel. Like Takashi, he first shows them how to make *tōchin* (pillows), a form they must perfect until they can advance to small plates and handleless cups. As they become more adept, they learn to throw more quickly, producing the desired shape in great number and with astonishing uniformity. Despite the frustration

James LaChance (Grotto Foundation Apprentice, 1993), *Paper Dolls*, 2000, cast iron, 48 3/4 in. wide. "I wanted to make a small monument to children after listening to Republicans talk about how more standardized testing will help them become better learners. They forgot to mention the real reasons like drugs, poverty, and single-parent homes. I wanted to show both the frailty and strength of children, so I made a paper-doll chain out of 300 pounds of iron."
Photograph by Robert Fogt, 2001.

he felt in Japan at having to take hundreds of objects to the stamper because they did not exactly replicate the models Takashi had provided, Bresnahan adheres to the same method. For with time, he realized such "discipline throwing" leads to an intuitive understanding of the clay itself—to a point where the potter no longer has to think about the object being thrown but does it instinctively and with great spontaneity.

"A common Japanese expression," writes Singleton, "refers to such bodily learning as *karada de oboeru* (learning by the body). It is a phrase that is regularly applied to potters at the wheel, *ama* [female divers] searching the reef for abalone, auto mechanics, and people explaining the significance of the practice forms (*kata*) of the martial arts" (Singleton, *Learning in Likely Places*, p. 16). Former apprentice Kevin Flicker recalls, "I heard that several apprentices had quit in disgust in the early stages of their 'throwing discipline' and had returned to their previous lives. But I was determined to persevere in this task. . . . Making the same form over and over again at times seemed very tedious but I understood how this repetitive throwing discipline would ultimately, paradoxically, result in the greater throwing freedom I desired."

Kevin Flicker (Grotto Foundation Apprentice, 1985), *Bell Jar*, 1999, stoneware with natural ash glaze, 16½ in. high. Although Flicker drew inspiration for this work from the shape of an ancient Thai pot, he altered the form so completely that this jar bears little resemblance to its prototype. "I strive for my pots to have a certain timeless quality. I have a great respect for ceramic traditions, but do not feel that old forms should be blindly reproduced for tradition's sake."
Photograph by Robert Fogt, 2001.

Despite his dependence on his Japanese experience, Bresnahan does vary his approach in some significant ways. He accepts the fact that most American students will only stay at the pottery for a year or two—a fraction of the time Japanese apprentices spend in training. To accommodate this, he has streamlined the process, enabling the apprentices to become informed about all aspects of operating a studio before they leave. By the time they depart, he also insists they attain a level of technical skill that will allow them to support themselves financially.

In the Japanese system, a master purposely refrains from divulging certain things until he deems his pupil ready and worthy to receive it. This slow parceling out of information also helps ensure that apprentices stay long enough for the studio to profit for the

"Through observing and participating, the artist in me emerged in a deeper way—a visionary way, a way of life, a way of breathing, a way of seeing, a way of speaking, a way of perceiving. I came to Saint John's to study theology and spirituality, but I also gained a precious gift because in my heart an artist was born and nurtured." Father Daniel Lenz (Grotto Foundation Apprentice, 1984–85) surrounded by some of his own clay sculptures.
Photograph by James R. Dean, 1989.

Father Daniel Lenz (Grotto Foundation Apprentice, 1984–85), *Madonna of Hospitality*, 1986, stoneware with elm ash glaze and natural fly ash, 23½ in. high. A member of the Benedictine community of Mount Michael Abbey near Elkhorn, Nebraska, Father Daniel apprenticed with Bresnahan in the mid-1980s. After returning to Mount Michael, he built a single-chamber kiln there with the help of his fellow monks and students. Like Bresnahan, he also excavates and processes his own clay from deposits he finds nearby.
Photograph by Robert Fogt, 2001.

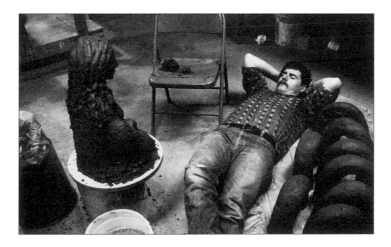

Daniel Siverson (Grotto Foundation Apprentice, 1996–98), *Rabbit*, **2000, stoneware, 26 in. long. After returning to Moorhead State University in 1998 to finish his degree, Siverson became increasingly interested in mixed-media assemblages. Recently, he went to Saint John's to help load and fire Bresnahan's kiln, and while there, he made this rabbit. He believes that the spirit of the place and the studio's commitment to natural materials influenced his decision to sculpt a wild animal.** Photograph by Robert Fogt, 2001.

expense and bother of training them. Moreover, Japanese masters typically do not overtly teach. "There is . . . a powerful pedagogy that depends upon the observational skills of a motivated learner," writes Singleton. "It is the ability to respond to 'teaching without teaching' and is personified in the learner or apprentice called a *minarai* [literally, learner by observation]. But it is the learner who has to puzzle out the ways in which unobtrusive observation and persistent stealth will be tolerated . . . in such a way that the necessary skills and practices will become evident" (Singleton, *Learning in Likely Places*, pp. 16–17).

In describing the problems he had while apprenticing with a Japanese potter and experiencing "teaching without teaching," Bill Haase writes: "Japanese craftsmen have often been characterized as *mukuchi* (taciturn, literally 'having no mouth')" (Haase, "Learning to Be an Apprentice," p. 109). The more an apprentice demonstrates patience and perseverance with these practices, the more respect is gained in the master's eyes. But Bresnahan instinctually knew this approach would prove difficult with American students, largely because of the vast cultural differences between Japan and the United States. Whereas the Japanese value conformity and a deference to authority, Americans laud individualism and a questioning of power. In addition, Bresnahan realized he could not reasonably expect Americans to commit to the prolonged apprenticeships typical in Japan when such traditions are not routine here.

Unwilling to compromise his standards, Bresnahan decided he needed to devise ways to train his apprentices within a shorter time frame. To this end, he has the apprentices attend to such labor-intensive tasks as processing clay, slip, and glazes during the day. As part of the pottery's open-door policy, they also give tours of the facility and explain Bresnahan's ecological philosophies to visitors. During work breaks, they gather around the studio's *irori* to exchange information, review the day's schedule, and socialize. They eat lunch together, too, at the university's refectory, where other students and professors often join them. And more advanced apprentices gain teaching experience by helping newer students.

In the evening, when the studio is closed to the public, the students practice throwing on the wheel. Unlike the hushed stillness of most Japanese potteries, Bresnahan's studio is awash with lively discussions. "Periodically during the day, and often at night," reports Stephen Earp, "Bresnahan would talk about any number of topics, from the history of early Japanese pottery, to pricing methods, to ways of scavenging for raw materials." At the same time, Bresnahan works at the wheel, giving the apprentices the opportunity to regularly observe him making an array of changing forms. "The knowledge I would take with me came from watching Richard create pottery," says 1994–95 apprentice Gabriel Stockinger, "what I saw was efficiency of motion, understanding limitations, maximizing results, pattern, repetition, attention to detail. In a word, balance."

Because Bresnahan emphasizes self-sufficiency in all things, he does not limit the assignments he gives to the inner workings of the studio. By gathering and

"It was difficult to maintain a pace of working that was so encompassing it allowed for little else. I had to adjust my living to that one purpose. But that focus is where learning occurred. When everything I did was related to . . . one thing, I came to understand that thing, and that was valuable." Daniel Siverson (Grotto Foundation Apprentice, 1996–98) making cups in the Saint John's studio. Bresnahan works nearby (foreground) as do apprentices Samuel Johnson and Katherine Mathieson.
Photograph by James R. Dean, 1997.

preparing the enormous quantity of wood needed for each firing, for example, every apprentice becomes adept at wielding a log splitter. Bresnahan also involves his students in useful projects outside the pottery, giving them lessons in what he calls "survival."

"The skills I developed went far beyond clay," says 1989 apprentice Paul Wegner. "The list is long and varied and includes logging, milling, building with wood, constructing energy-efficient heating and cooling systems, setting stone and tile, and building stone

"One of the most important concepts at the core of the Saint John's Pottery is Bresnahan's diligence regarding the utilization of local and sustainable materials. This is a goal of mine as well." David Swenson (Grotto Foundation Apprentice, 1984–85) applying white slip to some of his bowls.
Photograph by James R. Dean, 1989.

David Swenson (Grotto Foundation Apprentice, 1984–85), *Energy I*, 1998, wood and steel, 48 in. diameter. Swenson worked in clay during his apprenticeship with Bresnahan. But his great skill at using tools and mechanical abilities have led him to build finely crafted assemblages, often from a variety of materials.
Photograph by Robert Fogt, 2001.

terraces." By his own example, Bresnahan provides his students with alternatives, showing them how to be financially independent, maintain a sense of personal integrity, and create art true to themselves. Former apprentice Catherine Braun, when asked to recount the most valuable lesson she learned from Bresnahan, responded, "The key to life is being resourceful. There is a way to reuse anything in society for making something else."

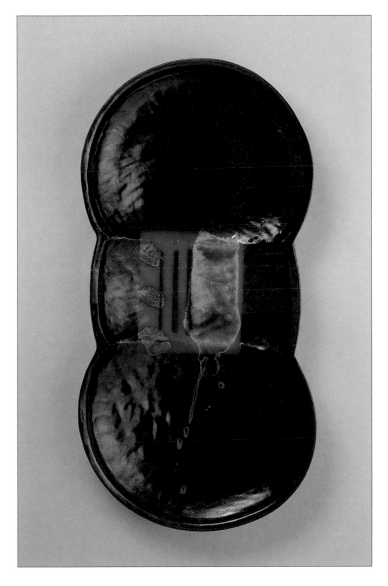

David Swenson (Grotto Foundation Apprentice, 1984–85), *Platter,* **1998, glazed earthenware with overglaze enamels, 26 in. high.**
Photograph by Robert Fogt, 2001.

Nevertheless, the sheer physicality of being a potter comes as a surprise to many. "I remember very clearly the first task Bresnahan set me to," recalls Stephen Earp, "screening by hand about seven tons of refractory clay he had recently come across in preparation for running tests on its usability. In addition, I was expected to foot-wedge sand into another fourteen tons of standard shop clay. Then I was put on that Korean-style kick wheel. I thought my legs would fall off. I could barely walk. But oddly enough, I was learning more in those first few weeks than I had in all the previous five years in college."

Most unanimously agree they left the studio far better equipped to pursue their goals than when they arrived. Even apprentices whose residencies last for only nine months usually acquire the necessary discipline and skill for production throwing. With this, they can then find employment at a commercial pottery studio if necessary while they explore their long-term options. And because Bresnahan encourages all of his apprentices to produce 800 to 900 plates, bowls, and mugs that they can sell, they also leave with a valuable inventory of their own work.

Over time, however, some apprentices feel overwhelmed by Bresnahan and the extent to which the studio dominates their lives. This is especially true in the months leading up to a firing, when the workload increases and takes on an even greater urgency. "Having your life revolve around the pottery studio was the most challenging part," notes Catherine Braun. "It wasn't a 9 to 5 job where you went home and

"I began to understand intelligence in a new way—it was more natural and closer than I once thought. Old knowledge and tradition brushed up against me daily, and my sense of time, history, and civilization all began to change. I began to understand myself as nature in a natural world. And through all this, the world—its cycle and beat—somehow became more pronounced and clear." Samuel Johnson (Grotto Foundation Apprentice, 1996–99) and Bresnahan (left) applying elm ash glaze to some cups.
Photograph by James R. Dean, 1999.

Samuel Johnson (Grotto Foundation Apprentice, 1996–99), *Jar*, 2000, low-fired porcelain with borax and iron glaze, 14 1/2 in. high. "While studying at the Royal Porcelain Factory in Copenhagen, I became interested in the chalky quality of porcelain that's only fired to around 1,100° centigrade—rather than the translucency that's possible at higher temperatures."
Photograph by Robert Fogt, 2001.

forgot about it." Consequently, the longer the apprentices stay, the more restless and isolated they sometimes feel. "My intention as Bresnahan's apprentice," says Samuel Johnson, whose three-year residency (1996–99) has been the longest so far, "was to quiet my own ego—to supplicate myself. It was a kind of self-achieved submission for the sake of study." Stephen Earp echoed this sentiment when he said: "It became, in a way, a question of how long I could hold my breath."

Of the twenty-eight people who have studied with Bresnahan at Saint John's, more than half have become professional potters and several others now teach at universities. Most agree the apprenticeship proved instrumental in their development and continues to impact how they see their craft. Some have even built wood-burning kilns, and nearly all believe in using sustainable natural resources. Many also cite Bresnahan's strong work ethic and boundless enthusiasm as indispensable qualities to succeeding as a practicing artist. "Make sure this is your passion before making the commitment," warns David Swenson (1984–85). Samuel Johnson offers similar advice by quoting songwriter Bob Dylan, "'playing for time is just horsing around.'"

Bresnahan's first Japanese apprentice, Yamaki Shumpei, joined the studio in January 2001. After Yamaki broke his arm in a car accident in 1998, his mother suggested he take a pottery class as a form of physical therapy. At the time, he was an international student at the University of Wisconsin in La Crosse. He first studied ceramics there under Karen Terpstra. Later, he went to the University of Iowa in Iowa City to work with Chuck Hindes and Donna Gilliss; they, in turn, suggested he apprentice at Saint John's with Richard Bresnahan.
Photograph by James Dean, April 2001.

Sugi Kazuaki (Jerome Foundation Emerging Artist, 1985–86, 1988–94) ritually purifying the area around the Johanna kiln with incense during the blessing on October 12, 1994.
Photograph by Laura A. Crosby, 1994.

Visiting Artists

Occasionally, while Richard Bresnahan was studying in Japan, artists would visit the Nakazatos, interrupting the studio's normal routine. Often, these guests had achieved success in creative disciplines other than pottery, and some had even been recognized as "Intangible Cultural Assets" or "Living National Treasures." Accordingly, Takashi would graciously welcome them, send Bresnahan or another assistant to prepare tea, and proceed to give a tour of the studio and the kiln.

Usually, Takashi would then invite his visitors to try their hand at clay. Despite their unfamiliarity with the material, most would enthusiastically roll up their sleeves and begin to experiment. Bresnahan always marveled at their lack of self-consciousness and willingness to play. Later, over dinner, he would listen as they described their own training, the challenges they faced, and their views on art, politics, and life. Surrounded by creative individuals who were deeply committed to their professions made Bresnahan feel spiritually nourished. As they shared stories, laughed, ate, and drank, he gained new insights and for days thereafter as he wedged clay or carried boards, he would mull over their conversations and, at least for a time, see things in different ways.

After setting up his own studio in Minnesota, Bresnahan went about creating the kind of environment he had enjoyed in Karatsu. When he met other artists, he would inevitably invite them to come to Saint John's. Those who accepted his offer often would find themselves shaping a mound of clay while Bresnahan worked nearby on his wheel. Attracted to the young potter's openness and vivacity, many would stay for a meal. During these occasions, Bresnahan discovered that sculptors, especially, had a sincere interest in his work. Many, in fact, wanted to discover ways to make their pieces more organic without applying colored enamels. As they talked, Bresnahan recalled his first impression of wood-fired ceramics—that Americans probably would not like their rough surfaces, irregular ash glazing, and earthy tonalities for tablewares. But such effects, he remembered thinking, could revolutionize sculpture in the United States, and that assessment was repeatedly confirmed by the sculptors who visited his Saint John's studio.

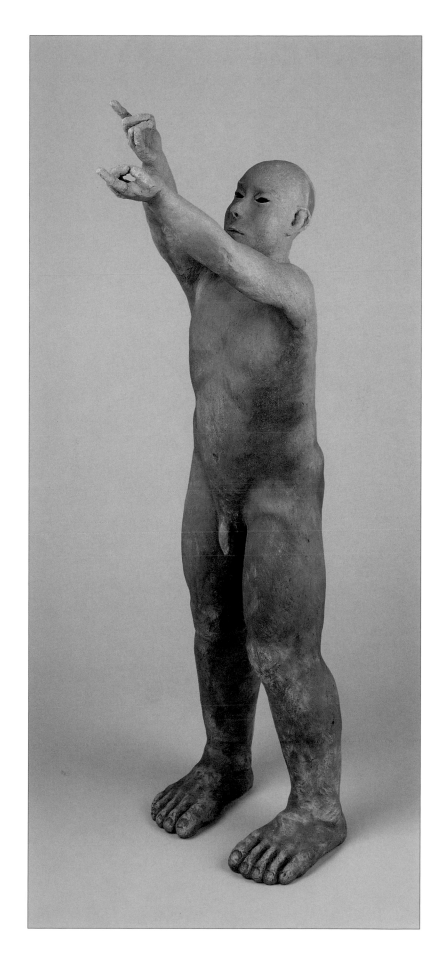

Sugi Kazuaki (Jerome Foundation Emerging Artist, 1985–86, 1988–94), *Pointing at the Moon,* **1988, stoneware, 49 in. high.**
Photograph by Robert Fogt, 2001.

Ann Klefstad (Jerome Foundation Emerging Artist, 1998), *Ancient Dog*, 1998, stoneware with natural ash glaze, 21½ in. high. Inspired by ancient Japanese tomb figures known as *haniwa*, Klefstad made a series of dogs characterized by their simplicity of form and ornamentation. Living on the edge of vast forests in northern Minnesota near the Canadian border, Klefstad chose to depict dogs because she sees them as a link between the domesticated world and the wild one.
Photograph by Robert Fogt, 2001.

Robin Murphy (Jerome Foundation Emerging Artist, 1988), *Untitled* (*Angel* series), 1988, stoneware with natural ash glaze and stones, 21¾ in. high. Trained as a ballerina, Murphy wanted to make clay sculptures suggesting the human body in motion. This work represents the dancer's arm movements—port de bras. She deliberately kept the form simple and the surface decor to a minimum so she could arrange the piece with other works to evoke the activated space that dancers create.
Photograph by Robert Fogt, 2001.

Karl Unnasch (Jerome Foundation Emerging Artist, 2000), *Tool Series: Vise Grip*, 1999, wood, metal, and clay, 63 in. wide. Unnasch has long been interested in tools and their place in human evolution. In this work, he enclosed a vise grip—a particularly sophisticated devise—in a split stick, a primitive implement that can either function as a club or a lever. He also included stone and clay fragments, suggesting the destructive use of tools to hack and bash.
Photograph by Robert Fogt, 2001.

"I think Bresnahan's work ethic had the greatest influence on me. I also gained more of an ability to focus on my work and knowledge about the wood-firing process." Anne-Bridget Gary (Jerome Foundation Emerging Artist, 1990) making one of her large clay figures.
Photograph by James R. Dean, 1990.

Anne-Bridget Gary (Jerome Foundation Emerging Artist, 1990), *figureform*, 1990, stoneware with white slip, 16 in. high. Faced with middle age, Gary created a series of semi-abstract fertility figures to celebrate the productive lives of women—not as bearers of children, but as maturing adults developing their own interests and skills.
Photograph by Robert Fogt, 2001.

With the working artists he met, Bresnahan discussed such subjects as conservation, pollution, and sustainability. Many were dismayed to learn that the ready-made supplies they regularly ordered from manufacturers often contributed to ecological degradation. Many of the materials they purchased, Bresnahan pointed out, also were extremely toxic. He encouraged them to follow his example and seek out methods that would not only reflect their artistic visions but safeguard their health and the natural world as well.

As Bresnahan talked to more people who seemed to take a genuine interest in his approach, he became convinced that his pottery and wood-burning kiln could become valuable community resources. Not only were there ceramists and sculptors who wanted to find alternatives to gas and electric kilns and industrially processed clay, but other artists who longed to broaden their creative vision by exploring a different medium. In 1982, he submitted a request to the Jerome Foundation in St. Paul, Minnesota,

asking for money to subsidize two-month stays at the pottery. Unlike the apprentices, he wrote, these artists would work independently of him but use the studio's materials and equipment to pursue their own goals. While he would be available to tell them about the nature of clay or to solve a particular problem they were having, these artists would be largely on their own. In turn, Bresnahan imagined that their unique knowledge and varied backgrounds would enhance the studio environment, both for himself and the apprentices.

The Jerome Foundation was founded by Jerome Hill, the younger brother of Louis W. Hill, Jr., and the grandson of James J. Hill, the railroad builder and lumber baron. After majoring in music at Yale University, Jerome Hill studied painting at the British Academy in Rome and the Académie Scandinav in Paris. He later turned his considerable talents to filmmaking, earning an Oscar in 1957 for a documentary on Albert Schweitzer. He used his substantial wealth to help fellow artists in Europe and the

"I think of the time at Saint John's as a turning point. I was headed for a life of university teaching. It was safe and what was expected of me. The voice I heard at the pottery was telling me to go elsewhere. I listened. I am on a much more personal path now." Frank Pitcher (Jerome Foundation Emerging Artist, 1984) inside the damp room of Bresnahan's original Saint John's studio.
Photograph by James R. Dean, 1984.

United States, often without their knowledge, and in 1964, he established the foundation to advance the careers of emerging artists in both Minnesota and New York City.

Starting in 1983, the Saint John's Pottery began receiving Jerome funds to support two to three artists for summer residencies. Since then, thirty men and women have participated in the program. As young

Frank Pitcher (Jerome Foundation Emerging Artist, 1984), *Figure*, 1984, stoneware, 21 in. high. Shortly after his arrival at Saint John's in 1984, Pitcher began creating simple figures with gaping mouths. He drew inspiration for these expressive creatures, in part, from hearing the monks singing during prayer services. The sculptures also represent his own open-mouthed, wide-eyed terror at the specter of nuclear war.
Photograph by Robert Fogt, 2001.

Annie Baggenstoss (Jerome Foundation Emerging Artist, 1999), *Ancestor* **(left) and** *Inspiration,* **1999, stoneware with natural ash glaze, 10 in. high (each). While at Saint John's, Baggenstoss visited the university's science department, which prompted her to sculpt these two skulls: one Neanderthal; the other, Homo sapiens. As a former medical student, Baggenstoss memorized, sketched, and labeled skeletal remains. She sees human skulls as beautiful forms, not as emblems of death.**
Photograph by Robert Fogt, 2001.

artists, most are familiar with the harsh realities of making a living by their craft, and many experience the difficulty of finding the time and resources to investigate new methods of creativity. Jerome Foundation grants make it possible for them to retreat to Saint John's for two months, live in the dormitories, eat at the student refectory, have a work space in the studio, gain access to unlimited quantities of clay, and receive a $3,000 stipend to cover other expenses.

Freed from their usual responsibilities, these artists typically immerse themselves in the experience with surprising intensity. "I was excited about a new body of work that had been brewing inside

me for some time," recalls Frank Pitcher (1984). "There were many nights I worked straight through, would go outside and watch the sun come up, then go back in and work until breakfast. I'd catch a few hours of sleep afterwards, then return to the studio." For many, the opportunity to devote themselves entirely to their art proved unusual. "Besides creating, all you have to do is your laundry!" exclaimed Jennifer Lorge (1999) to incoming artist Annie Baggenstoss (1999). "I desperately needed time away from my day job to pursue art-making in depth," states Jane Frees-Kluth (2000). "It was the first time I was able to fully focus on my personal artistic development."

Since the program is open to anyone who is interested in clay's creative possibilities, many visiting artists at the studio handle the material for the first time. In fact, in addition to ceramists, participants have included painters, printmakers, sculptors of stone and metal, a glass blower, and even a textile artist. Some spend the first half of their residency just experimenting. "When I discovered clay could stretch, I went nuts doing bulbous shapes," recalls Jennifer Lorge. "After one particularly industrious night making large forms, I was deflated the next day when I went to the damp room and discovered the effects of gravity." Sculptor John Running-Johnson (1984) also had

Jennifer Lorge (Jerome Foundation Emerging Artist, 1999), *For Father Peregrin* (left), 2000, mica, stoneware, and found objects, 9 in. high, and *Asp Coffin*, 1999, stoneware with natural ash glaze, 9 in. high. When doctors told Jennifer Lorge that her husband probably would die from heart complications, she started constructing miniature coffins. Made from mica and found objects, the coffins, says Lorge, signify hope and resurrection, not death. At Saint John's, she fashioned more coffins out of clay. She adorned *Asp Coffin* with snakes, a traditional symbol of fertility that for the artist represents femininity. Because snakes shed their skins, they also stand for rebirth and healing. Photograph by Robert Fogt, 2001.

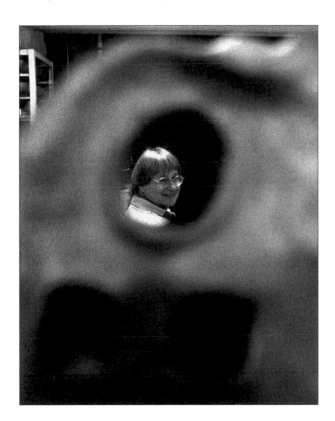

"I know that if I am given time in a studio, I can be very productive. I have 273 wood-fired pieces from my two months at Saint John's. I have rediscovered my desire and the drive to create." Jennifer Lorge (Jerome Foundation Emerging Artist, 1999) seen through an opening in one of her clay sculptures. Photograph by James R. Dean, 1999.

difficulty using clay initially. "When working in a material as strong as steel," he writes, "it is nothing to forge one element onto another, immediately building up structure, never having to wait for it to gain strength, always proceeding to the next move as instinct dictates. I soon realized, as I watched my clay forms collapse before my eyes, that not only was I addicted to a certain rhythm, but that my ideas, spatial ideas in particular, emanated from that rhythm."

While at Saint John's, most artists also find that the high level of activity at the studio leads them to greater productivity. "The experience honed my skills in the

John Running-Johnson (Jerome Foundation Emerging Artist, 1984), *Choo-Choo Truth*, **1989, painted and stained steel, wood, and bronze, 12 in. high. "I get the greatest satisfaction by creating forms that have an ambiguous appearance. I am fascinated by the implication of motion that a still object can have."**
Photograph by Robert Fogt, 2001.

"We got into a working routine that did not exactly start at the crack of dawn, but often lasted until the wee hours of the morning. Being at Saint John's and only having to engage in the pursuit of the next piece was liberating. As the summer moved along, each working day became a treasure." John Running-Johnson (Jerome Foundation Emerging Artist, 1984) with Bresnahan (center) and Frank Pitcher (right).
Photograph by James R. Dean, 1984.

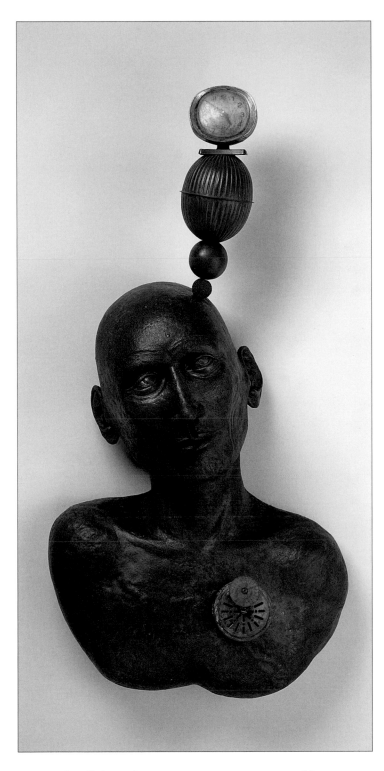

James A. Jones (Jerome Foundation Emerging Artist, 1985), *Heartfelt*, 2000, clay, paint, and found objects, 34 in. high. "Because the bust contains the heart and the head, I find it very expressive of the archetypal struggles of human beings. The found objects I incorporate into my work are discards from everyday life. Here, a rubber ball, a round wooden finial, an old toilet float, and a clock create a thought bubble about time. The perforated metal disk is part of an old respirator, but I wanted to convey the idea that everyone would be better off if they listened to their hearts. The compass has always intrigued me as a device for helping us find our way. By listening to our hearts, we may find our true purpose in life." Photograph by Robert Fogt, 2001.

"The experience honed my self-discipline, time management, and adaptability to new environments, people, and schedules. I also gained an understanding of the wood-firing process and its applications. I learned the importance of working cooperatively in a small community of artists toward the common goal of making work for the firing." James A. Jones (Jerome Foundation Emerging Artist, 1985) working on one of his large clay sculptures. Photograph by James R. Dean, 1985.

areas of self-discipline, time management, and being able to adapt quickly to new environments, people, and schedules," observes James A. Jones (1985). "I learned the importance of working cooperatively in a small community of artists toward the common goal of making work for the firing."

David Alban (Jerome Foundation Emerging Artist, 1985), *Self as Eleven-Headed Kannon,* **1998, glazed earthenware, 42 in. high. Alban modeled this self-portrait after Kannon, a benevolent Buddhist demigod whose eleven heads symbolize the final stages of its progress toward enlightenment. Rather than showing the heads as part of an elaborate crown, which would have been a typical Buddhist representation, Alban sculpted them in various sizes and locations, as if spontaneously erupting from the largest one.**
Photograph by Robert Fogt, 2001.

Moreover, the ready availability of vast amounts of clay and glazes inspires many artists as well. Bresnahan typically welcomes new arrivals with a tour of the facility; after showing them their work space, he then points out a wooden box in the center of the studio that holds two tons of processed clay and an adjacent storage room with an additional twenty tons. He concludes his introduction with a simple statement: "There it is. Go for it." For artists who usually purchase clay in twenty-pound sacks, the immense quantities of free materials seem both staggering and inspiring. "Within twenty minutes," Bresnahan recalls, "David Alban (1985) was hard at work. I think he went through nine tons of clay that summer."

The communal atmosphere of the studio also offers the artists a chance to learn from others. "I would pick the brains of the apprentices for information and demonstrations of how to do certain things in clay," says Jennifer Lorge. "I was new to clay and it took the first month just to get to know it." Bresnahan laughingly adds that many visiting artists avoid asking him questions to conceal their lack of knowledge, even though as practitioners in other mediums he would

David Alban (Jerome Foundation Emerging Artist, 1985) seated before ten tons of clay in the pottery's settling tank.
Photograph by James R. Dean, 1985.

James Loftus (Jerome Foundation Emerging Artist, 1986),
***Vase,* 1987, stoneware, 17 in. high.**
Photograph by Robert Fogt, 2001.

never expect them to know about clay. Nevertheless, they often feel more comfortable questioning the apprentices when Bresnahan is not in the studio. But even that has an added bonus. "Teaching helps build the apprentices' confidence," Bresnahan explains. "Suddenly they realize they have a lot to offer. They are no longer the studio's neophytes."

At the same time, the apprentices benefit from watching other artists find solutions to their aesthetic dilemmas.

Painter James Loftus (Jerome Foundation Emerging Artist, 1986) struggled on the potter's wheel before deciding to make his pieces from cut slabs of clay, which he then incised. Here, he poses with some of the work he created at the Saint John's Pottery.
Photograph by James R. Dean, 1987.

For some, seeing others struggle makes them realize that artists are not mystic seers who achieve success effortlessly. The environmental artist Danielle Callahan (2000), for example, spent weeks walking Saint John's grounds and interviewing monks before she felt she could interpret the place creatively. Painter James Loftus (1986) had a miserable time on the potter's wheel until he decided to dispense with it altogether and use a slab technique instead for his incised two-dimensional pieces. Similarly, John Running-Johnson refused to be constrained by his lack of skill on the wheel and pinched rolled slabs of clay together to achieve the tall cylinders he wanted. However, when sculptor Joseph Samuelson (1987) built a form over a chicken-wire armature, the work cracked severely in the kiln. But even that failure proved to be a good learning experience, both for Samuelson and the entire studio.

Interacting with artists makes the apprentices aware of the difficulties they, too, will face to practice their craft: the high cost of studio space, the demands of spouses and children, and the time-consuming effort of exhibiting and selling their work. The respect artists show in handling their pieces also can be revelatory. Jane Frees-Kluth, for example, surprised the apprentices when she hired a model to pose for her, then later carefully catalogued her sculptures and had them professionally photographed.

"I was becoming interested in physiology and anatomy, both scientifically and artistically, and developing a personal approach to sculpting the human figure in all its miraculous and quirky ways." Jane Frees-Kluth (Jerome Foundation Emerging Artist, 1999) works while Bresnahan talks to the model of her sculpture *Quadruped*.
Photograph by James R. Dean, 1999.

Jane Frees-Kluth (Jerome Foundation Emerging Artist, 1999), *Big Lucky*, 1999, stoneware with natural ash glaze, 12 in. high. When Frees-Kluth began exploring ways to portray the human figure, she looked at sculptures from both the Western world and the East. For this work, she decided to take a whimsical approach. While considering pregnancy, she had seen images of Ganesha, the Hindu god of wisdom, who is always represented with an elephant's head. She then made this robust fertility figure, adding Ganesha's head to a coquettishly posed female body.
Photograph by Robert Fogt, 2001.

Jane Frees-Kluth (Jerome Foundation Emerging Artist, 1999), *Man of Many Men*, 1999, stoneware, 54 in. high. The complex interplay of emotions, moods, and thoughts that comprise each individual prompted Frees-Kluth to sculpt the lower half of a human body as an aggregate of many people. Depending on the viewer's own state of mind, the small figures could be clambering into a cohesive whole or disintegrating into a heap of disparate entities.

Photograph by Robert Fogt, 2001.

"The firing was something. We started together with a little fire in the front, as if sitting around a campfire. Then we had shifts. Mine was double since it was during the day. Sometimes people would come around and throw a log on. Other times it was just you and the kiln. By the end of the week, when we got to the last chamber, Joe and I were working together throwing wood. The flames were flying." Julie Ravins Byers (Jerome Foundation Emerging Artist, 1987) with Joseph Samuelson stoking the Takigama kiln.

Photograph by James R. Dean, 1987.

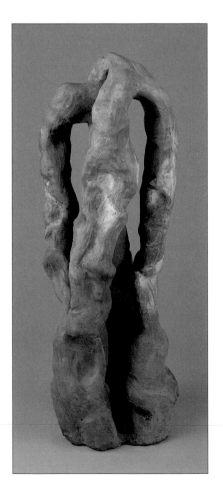

Julie Ravins Byers (Jerome Foundation Emerging Artist, 1987), *Loops of Friends*, 1987, stoneware, 38 in. high. "Before going to Saint John's, I was working on treelike forms inspired by the twisted and gnarled shapes of oak branches. Through wood firing, I discovered that I could achieve natural colors without the application of slips and glazes."

Photograph by Robert Fogt, 2001.

Joseph Samuelson (Jerome Foundation Emerging Artist, 1987), *Lear's Fool*, 1987, stoneware with natural ash glaze, 22 3/4 in. high. The natural ash glazes and kiln encrustations that appear on works fired in Bresnahan's climbing kiln reminded Samuelson of the hoary quality of newly excavated Greek and Roman statuary. While working at the pottery, he studied books on ancient art and then produced his own series of sculptures based on historic and literary figures. This one, called *Lear's Fool*, possesses the mottled surface texture he desired, which resulted from placing the work in the last chamber of the Takigama kiln.

Photograph by Robert Fogt, 2001.

Catherine Mulligan (Jerome Foundation Emerging Artist, 1983 and 1997), *Vessel—The Voyage*, 1997, stoneware with natural ash glaze, 8½ in. high. After reading about the 18th-century British slave trade, Mulligan began thinking about the human obsession with wealth and power. Greed, especially, helped fuel the slave trade, causing the subjugation of countless people who were kidnapped from their homelands and transported like cargo across the sea. Here, Mulligan suggested the plight of women in such circumstances by placing two fertility figures in a small boat. Ironically, the prow of the boat also has been outfitted with a female figurehead; two oars lie uselessly inside the vessel.
Photograph by Robert Fogt, 2001.

Still other artists come with such indomitable spirits that everyone becomes inspired. Jennifer Lorge arrived at the studio with the stated purpose of rediscovering her lost creativity, which had become nearly extinct over the previous seven years while she cared for her seriously ill husband. And sculptor Catherine Mulligan (1983 and 1997) brought a rare sense of humanity with her, nurturing and encouraging everyone she met, without regard for their background or position at the studio.

Each artist's residency at the pottery ultimately results in a myriad of works that will be fired in the wood-burning kiln. Since firings usually occur in the fall, many artists return to help load and stoke the kiln. Most agree, however, that they left Saint John's with much more than clay ceramics and sculpture. "The experience gave me a sense of confidence in doing my work and a determination to follow through and complete the projects I start," says Margaret Breimhurst (1991). "I look back to that point-in-time and it still gives me stamina and the courage to continue making art."

"All kinds of people do all kinds of things, but very few are so focused and have the vision, energy, and tenacity to build a community, and I really admire Bresnahan for that." Catherine Mulligan (Jerome Foundation Emerging Artist, 1983 and 1997) working on a clay figurine.
Photograph by James R. Dean, 1983.

Megan Sweeney (Jerome Foundation Emerging Artist, 1986) working on one of her sculptures.

Photograph by James R. Dean, 1986.

Megan Sweeney (Jerome Foundation Emerging Artist, 1986), *In the Counting House,* **stoneware with slip and black copper oxide, 27 in. high. To subsidize their incomes, many artists need to take jobs unrelated to their craft. Sweeney once had a position as an accounting clerk. The experience, as alien to her as it might have been to a monkey, prompted her to sculpt this figure. Covered with haphazard numerals and tallies, this whimsical primate seems both confused and amused.**

Photograph by Robert Fogt, 2001.

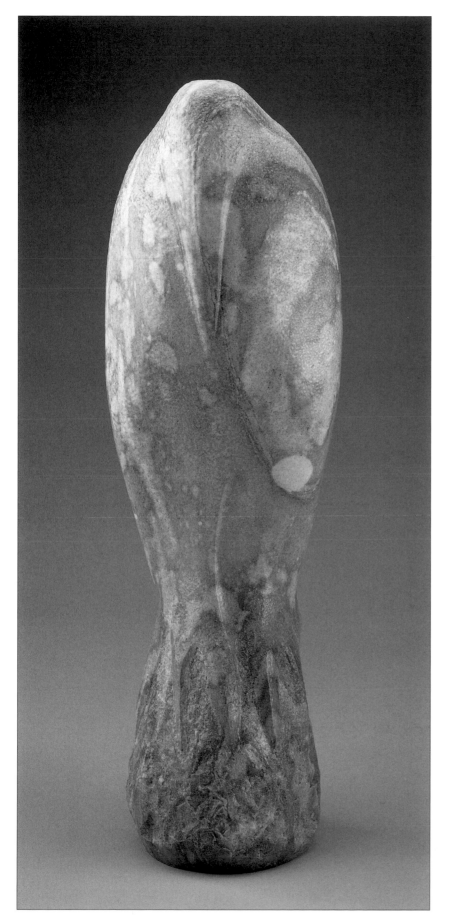

"Clay, which I was drawn to because of its plasticity, completed the circle of fire, color, texture, and process that had attracted me to bronze casting." Tadd Jensen (Jerome Foundation Emerging Artist, 1989) near the Takigama kiln.
Photograph by James R. Dean, 1990.

Tadd Jensen (Jerome Foundation Emerging Artist, 1989), *Egret*, 1989, pink quartzite with ash glaze, 25 in. high. Tadd Jensen made this sculpture from pink quartzite, one of the few rocks that can withstand extremely hot temperatures and not shatter. In the heat of the kiln, the natural silica content of the stone fluxes and then interacts with the natural fly ash to produce a transparent celadon glaze.
Photograph by Robert Fogt, 2001.

Kristin Plucar (Jerome Foundation Emerging Artist, 2000), *Untitled*, 2000, stoneware, 6 in. high. "I initially found inspiration in Buddhist stupas, which combine the circle and square as representations of heaven and earth. The carved openwork patterns on this piece recall the repetition found in painted mandalas, chanted mantras, and nature itself. I began with these basic ideas, but in the creative process the work developed independently."
Photograph by Robert Fogt, 2001.

Danielle Callahan (Jerome Foundation Emerging Artist, 2000), *Egg Stalk*, 2000, stoneware with natural ash glaze and stones, 24 1/2 in. high. Callahan often incorporates stones of various kinds in her mixed-media assemblages. While at Saint John's, she learned from Bresnahan that pink quartzite could tolerate firing at high temperatures, which led her to sculpt this plantlike form with its quartzite thorns.
Photograph by Robert Fogt, 2001.

For many artists, the experience at the studio becomes life affirming. Many adopt Bresnahan's environmental awareness, and still others learn how to better integrate their personal lives with their artistic careers. Bresnahan's children frequently come to the studio, and visiting artists have sometimes brought their own families with them to Saint John's. Such interactions make the apprentices realize that they, too, can have complicated existences and still be artists. "Bresnahan doesn't compartmentalize creativity," writes Danielle Callahan, "it's not just a visual thing. He's such a model for acknowledging the interconnectedness of all things." Kristin Plucar (2000) echoed this sentiment by saying, "The most valuable thing I learned is that 'community' is not just an abstract idea."

Many volunteers, working in six-hour shifts around-the-clock for ten days, help fire Bresnahan's wood-burning kiln. Here, the crew that assisted with the fifth firing of the Johanna kiln gathers for a commemorative portrait.
Photograph by James R. Dean, 2000.

The Artful Life

The creative spirit creates with whatever materials are present. With food, with children, with building blocks, with speech, with thoughts, with pigment, with an umbrella or a wineglass, or a torch. We are not craftsmen only during studio hours. Any more than a man is wise only in his library. Or devout only in church. The material is not the sign of the creative feeling for life: of the warmth and sympathy and reverence which foster being; techniques are not the sign; "art" is not the sign. The sign is the light that dwells within the act, whatever its nature or its medium.

— M. C. Richards

Pitcher (Johanna kiln, glaze chamber), 1998, stoneware with a navy-bean straw ash glaze, 9 7/8 in. high. Bresnahan credits the remarkable evenness of color and fineness of the "hare's fur" on many of his glazed wares to his apprentices, who carefully wash and rewash the ashes used for glaze mixtures. The controlled, slow cooling of the glaze chamber, which occurs over ten days, also allows the minerals in the glazes to continue to migrate and form the distinctive striations on the pieces.
Photograph by Gary Mortensen.

Opposite page: Bresnahan with his son, Richard III, and daughter Margaret Adelaide in his first studio at Saint John's. Bresnahan has always welcomed children into the pottery and takes an active interest in their unaffected opinions about ceramics.
Photograph by Michael Crouser, 1989.

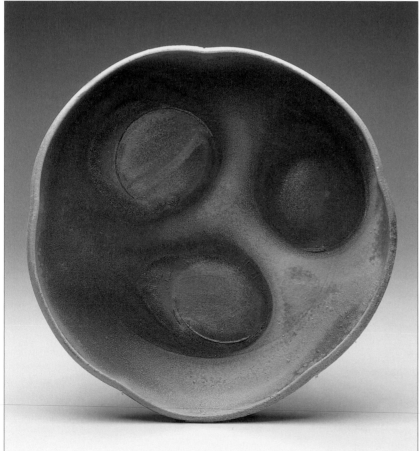

Five-footed melon-shaped plate and three spiral cups (Johanna kiln, Tanegashima chamber), 1998, stoneware, 10 1/2 in. diameter (plate), 3 1/2 in. high (cups). Using wild rice hulls as a buffer, Bresnahan placed this plate on top of three cups in the kiln, which made the circular patterns on the plate's surface. The irregular shapes of the circles and the color gradations between them reveal the dynamic movement of the flames during the firing.

Photograph by Gary Mortensen.

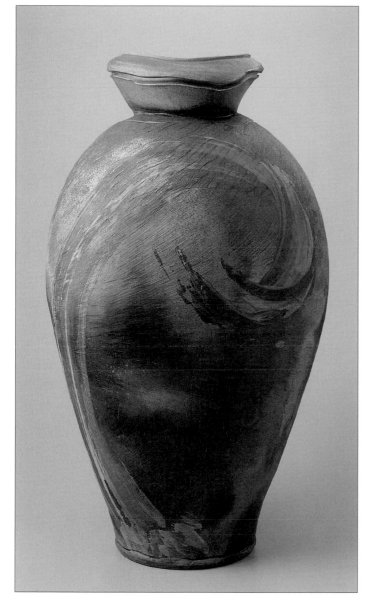

Large jar **(Johanna kiln, Tanegashima chamber), 1995, stoneware with slip painting, 38 in. high. Bresnahan gives his large jars visual interest by paddling the damp clay with carved mallets and then finger painting them with a porcelaneous slip. During the firing, the flames impart additional patterns and colors as they interact with the pots.**
Photograph by Gary Mortensen.

James Dean

In late fall 1981, a group of artists and collectors gathered at the Treetop Room, a restaurant in Moorhead, Minnesota. They had been at the Plains Art Museum, where an exhibition of Richard Bresnahan's ceramics had just opened. Among them was an architect and photographer named James Dean, who had driven three-and-a-half hours from St. Paul, Minnesota, to see the show and to meet the 27-year-old potter whom a friend—photographer Mark Strand—had spoken so highly of. Dean had been pleasantly surprised by the exhibit, and although he knew little about pottery, Bresnahan's work seemed both beautiful and honest to him. He also was impressed that someone so young had already accomplished so much.

When Bresnahan finally arrived later that evening, conversation between the two men came easily. Dean had grown up in Willmar, Minnesota, 52 miles southwest of St. Cloud, and his wife came from

Canisters (Johanna kiln, Tanegashima chamber), 1999, stoneware with slip painting, 11 7/8 in. high (left), 11 11/16 in. high (right). Works placed in the first row of the third chamber of the Johanna kiln take on unique surface effects when whole green logs, some five inches in diameter and seven feet long, are slid between them. Moisture from the wood reacts with the intense heat of the kiln to create the deep grays and iridescent blacks seen on these canisters.
Photograph by Gary Mortensen.

Casselton, North Dakota, Bresnahan's hometown. As Dean and Bresnahan talked, they discovered they both shared a distrust of government, an admiration for Bob Dylan, and a love of rural living. Dean, who was trying to establish a small architectural firm in St. Paul, had a degree from North Dakota State University and liked the ideas of Frank Lloyd Wright and such Bauhaus architects as Walter Gropius and Marcel Breuer. Like them, he believed that form should follow function and that good design need not be prohibitively expensive. Bresnahan's well-crafted, utilitarian wares accorded well with Dean's sense of modern design and their unadorned surfaces with his admiration for the simple and direct.

For his part, Bresnahan was struck by the sensitivity and modesty of the big man who sat across the table from him. In the previous five years, Dean had helped design two multimillion-dollar buildings in Bismarck, North Dakota—the North Dakota Heritage Center and a vocational school at the United Tribes Educational Training Center. He also had published two books of his photographs, had been given two solo exhibitions of his images, and was one of seven photographers chosen for a federally funded project to document the people and places of North Dakota. But Bresnahan found out these things later and from other people.

Teapot (Johanna kiln, front fire chamber), 1995, stoneware with natural ash glaze, 6 3/4 in. high. Reed handle by Paul Krueger. In a unique collaboration, sculptor Paul Krueger has been making handles for Bresnahan's teapots since 1981. Krueger carefully selects the colors of the reeds and the patterns he uses to complement the hues and shapes of each teapot.
Photograph by Gary Mortensen.

Like Bresnahan, Dean was concerned about humanity's negative impact on the earth. He was especially critical of architects and homeowners who built houses with little regard for their natural surroundings. When Bresnahan went to Dean's office a few weeks later, he discovered an excerpt from T. C. McLuhan's *Touch the Earth* taped to the wall. The quote, by a holy Wintu woman, lamented the destruction of the land and read: "The White people never cared for land or deer or bear. . . . How can the spirit of the earth like the White man? . . . Everywhere the White man has touched it, it is sore." During that same visit, Bresnahan learned that Dean was unhappy with city life and its dehumanizing effects.

But as Dean talked that night in Moorhead—not about money or possessions or impressive buildings—but about his own heartfelt ideas about architecture,

Francis Schellinger befriended Bresnahan soon after the young potter arrived at Saint John's and led him to the large deposit of local clay—some 18,000 tons—that Bresnahan still uses in his studio. Trained as a carpenter, Schellinger also taught Bresnahan about lumbering and milling. Here, he poses on top of his portable lumber mill.
Photograph by James R. Dean, June 1988.

Canister (Johanna kiln, front fire chamber), 1995, stoneware with natural ash glaze, 13 1/2 in. high.
Photograph by Gary Mortensen.

photography, and the natural environment, Bresnahan knew he had met a kindred spirit. He also sensed he had found someone who could help him realize his own dreams. For the past two years, he had been spending time with Francis Schellinger, learning how to mill wood. One day, when Schellinger came across a stand of trees on his land infected with Dutch elm disease, he offered to give Bresnahan the lumber if he helped fell and mill the trees. Together they cut the wood into massive 16-foot-long beams, which Bresnahan carefully stored on Schellinger's property, hoping one day they would form the core of his own house. But beyond such dreams, Bresnahan lacked the expertise to design a building and draft the plans. He needed an architect for that—and sitting there that night with James Dean he knew he had found the right person.

Over the next several months, Dean visited Bresnahan on several occasions, drawn to his new friend's energy and passion for art and life. Not only did Bresnahan have an admirable vision about how pottery should be made, but he enthusiastically conversed about other art forms as well. The two men talked about architecture and photography but also about painting, sculpture, music, and dance. They discussed regional politics and the growing plight of farmers in the Upper Midwest. Each time, Bresnahan introduced Dean to an ever-widening circle of people, many of whom were also artists. As the conversations lasted late into the night, Dean often was too tired to make the long drive back to St. Paul and would end up sleeping on Bresnahan's living-room floor. Dean's visits with Bresnahan also

In 1983, Colette and Richard Bresnahan, together with their friend James Dean (left), purchased 120 acres of densely wooded land near Saint John's University.
Photograph by James R. Dean, November 1983.

gave him the means to temporarily escape from his own troubles in the city. His marriage had recently failed, and after three years of hard work and sacrifice, his practice still had not turned a profit. Solace for Dean came in two forms: alcohol and trips to Collegeville.

Finally, in 1983, after numerous discussions with Dean, his business partner and longtime friend, Joel Davy, decided to move to California and start a new life. Ironically, just days before Davy and his family left, Dean got a sizable check in the mail. His father, although of modest means, had decided to give his two sons their inheritance while he was still alive. After the initial shock, Dean was jubilant. The unexpected gift meant relief from his financial woes: it

meant keeping the business afloat a while longer. It meant decent food, back rent on his tiny apartment, and badly needed car repairs.

A few days after Dean received the money, Bresnahan called, unaware of his good fortune. One hundred and twenty acres of dense hardwood forest just north of Saint John's were for sale. The owner insisted the parcel be kept intact, but Bresnahan and his bride-to-be could not manage the purchase alone. Would Dean be interested in the venture? Would he consider becoming a partner? Would he want to live in the woods? Dean asked Davy for his opinion. His friend did not hesitate with a response: "What else do you have going for you?" Without driving to Collegeville or even seeing a photograph of the property, Dean endorsed his father's check, sealed it in an envelope, and mailed it to Bresnahan.

"Nature Leaves Humans Behind" platter (Johanna kiln, glaze chamber), 1998, stoneware with white slip and iron painting under a basswood ash glaze, 13 ¼ in. diameter. To create the brushed pattern on this platter, Bresnahan used one of his favorite tools—an old whisk broom that someone else had discarded. Bresnahan's steadfast commitment to recycling and the environment earned him and the pottery the Business for Social Responsibility–Earth Day Award in 1996.

Photograph by Gary Mortensen.

Flat-sided bottle (Johanna kiln, glaze chamber), 1995, stoneware with sunflower-seed hull ash glaze over slip painting, 11 in. high. For centuries, Chinese and Korean potters decorated their flat-sided bottles and flasks with painted images. Bresnahan brushed on the abstract designs here with a thick porcelain slip and then coated the bottle with an ash glaze made from sunflower-seed hulls. Streaked with iron, the golden glaze covers the vessel so completely that only subtle undulations of the pattern can be seen on the surface.
Photograph by Gary Mortensen.

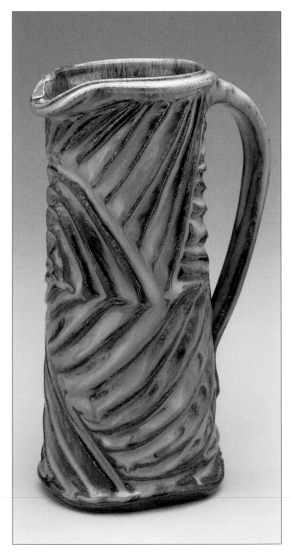

Plowed-field pitcher (Johanna kiln, glaze chamber), 1998, stoneware with iron slip under a navy-bean straw ash glaze, 9 1/8 in. high. Before glazing this pitcher, Bresnahan brushed the surface of the pot with an iron-rich slip to accentuate its carved pattern. During the firing, the glaze liquefied and settled into the furrows, while the iron in the slip burned through at the ridges, coloring them brown.
Photograph by Gary Mortensen.

Flat-sided bottle (Johanna kiln, glaze chamber), 1999, stoneware with porcelain slip, iron slip, flax-straw ash glaze, and elm ash glaze. 10 1/4 in. high. For some works, Bresnahan first paints the body of the vessel with an iron slip and then applies decoration with porcelain slip. Next, he ladles a viscous flax-straw ash glaze over the iron-slip areas and paints an elm ash glaze over the porcelain designs. During the firing, the two glazes flux and run together, revealing the decorations beneath them differently, like a mysterious veil through which shapes appear and recede.
Photograph by Gary Mortensen.

In all of his endeavors, Bresnahan has had the tireless support of his wife, Colette. As a registered nurse, she has always provided the family with a steady source of income. She is equally adept at operating a log splitter, planer, and chain saw. Here, Colette holds Margaret Adelaide, the Bresnahans' first-born daughter.
Photograph by James R. Dean, July 1988.

Colette Bresnahan

A year after he returned from Japan, Bresnahan met a nursing student at the College of Saint Benedict named Colette Wurtz. "She was incredibly beautiful and mysterious and totally unaware of it," Bresnahan recalls. "But even more than that, she had the most positive energy of anyone I had ever met." During their first encounter, Bresnahan got into a fierce argument with one of Colette's roommates about art. It was Colette who intervened, humored the combatants, and skillfully redirected the conversation to a more neutral topic.

In fact, even at the tender age of 19, Colette was already wise in the ways of peacemaking. She was the second child—and first daughter—in a family of ten children. Her father was a psychology professor at the University of Wisconsin in Menomonie, and her mother, a nurse. Colette often helped her mother, taking care of her younger brothers and sisters and developing a maternal patience and thoughtfulness while she herself was still a girl.

Bresnahan also admired Colette's commitment to her profession. She declined as many of his invitations as she accepted, and he quickly learned she was a dedicated and focused student. As they continued to date, he found they had other things in common as well. At a time when many young college-educated Americans were deciding not to have babies, they were each unequivocal about their desire for children. Both came from large families and had been raised in agricultural communities. But because neither of their parents had made a living from the land, they had somewhat sentimental ideas about rural living. Both wanted to replicate that lifestyle while pursuing their individual careers.

Although she did like the simplicity of his ceramics, Colette was not impressed with Bresnahan's status as a potter. If anything, her perception that artists were irresponsible and led unsettled, dissolute lives acted against him. She was equally unmoved by the exoticism of his Japanese apprenticeship. But she did respect the tremendous effort he went through to process his own materials instead of buying them. She also appreciated his commitment to the environment and the fact that he was "making a go at it himself."

Eventually, Bresnahan's staunch work ethic and genuine concern for family and friends won her over. She came to see in him a man whose desire for stability was as strong as her own and with whom she could raise a family and build a life. His boyish charm and ready smile also helped. As did his lively sense of humor. So when he proposed, she accepted and became Colette Bresnahan on June 11, 1983.

Double-gourd teapot (Johanna kiln, front fire chamber), 1999, stoneware with iron slip and natural ash glaze, 6 in. high. Reed handle by Paul Krueger. Part of the excitement of wood firing comes from its unpredictability. Wares from the front fire chamber can become lightly speckled with natural ash glaze or nearly encased in glassy rivulets. Here, the ash glaze formed an irregular curtain of color around the body of the teapot.
Photograph by Gary Mortensen.

"Nebulae" platter (Johanna kiln, front fire chamber), 1998, stoneware with natural ash glaze, 18 in. diameter. The amorphous shapes of interstellar clouds known as nebulae inspired Bresnahan to create a series of platters. To achieve the irregular edges on these pieces, he threw them with one hand, using a *hera* tool. He formed the concentric rings by pressing clay onto the center of each platter as it revolved on the potter's wheel.

Photograph by Gary Mortensen.

"Millennia bowl" (Johanna kiln, Tanegashima chamber), 2000, stoneware with porcelain and iron slip painting, 13 ¾ in. diameter. Bresnahan discovered that sturdy bowls like this, which he inverts and fires upside down, survive well in the Tanegashima chamber, where wood is tossed in from above and can sometimes damage the lips of more fragile vessels. Sister Johanna Becker dubbed these pots "Millennia bowls" because Bresnahan first made them in large numbers in the year 2000.

Photograph by Gary Mortensen.

Bresnahan working at the potter's wheel.
Photograph by James R. Dean, February 1996.

Tea bowl **(Johanna kiln, glaze chamber), 1995, stoneware with a navy-bean straw ash glaze, 2 1/2 in. high, 5 1/8 in. diameter.**
Photograph by Gary Mortensen.

The Master Plan

"My land is going to be perfect for you," announced the visitor to the pottery studio after Bresnahan had given him a tour. A retired school teacher from Annandale, Minnesota, Rudy Grunloh had a parcel of land once owned by his father near Saint John's University. When a neighbor in town tore down an old garage, Grunloh hauled the discarded lumber to his land and built a small, one-room cabin, fondly calling it his "tree house." He outfitted it with a corncob stove, planted irises and peonies outside, and hung a few birdhouses in the nearby trees. Located deep in the forest and only accessible by hiking up a steep gorge, the cabin was a closely kept secret that only a few locals knew about. For decades—from the spring thaw until the first snows each year—Grunloh had spent weekends and holidays in his private retreat in the woods.

But as he got older and his health began to fail, Grunloh made fewer trips to his property. His grown children lived in California and had little interest in it, so he began to think about selling it. For a few years, he postponed the inevitable, worried that developers would cut down the trees, level the hillocks, and build housing divisions there. But when the owner

of the local hardware store mentioned that Bresnahan was looking for some land, Grunloh decided to visit the studio. Bresnahan's talk about responsible use of natural materials must have met with Grunloh's approval for he invited the young potter to accompany him to the site that very afternoon.

Bresnahan could hardly contain his excitement as they wandered through the woods, where poplar, maple, oak, basswood, ironwood, and elm shaded the ground and made the air cool, even in August. Years before, Grunloh had planted saplings around his cabin, and now those pines towered as high as

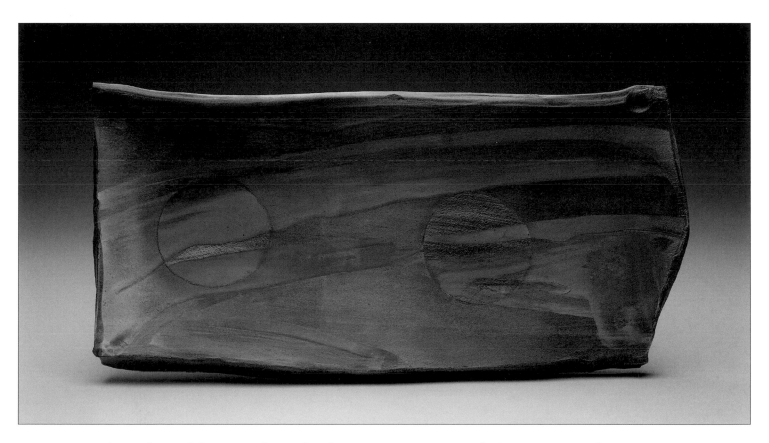

"Two Moon" plate (Johanna kiln, Tanegashima chamber), 1999, stoneware with slip painting, 15 3/4 in. wide. For many years, Bresnahan has painted his large jars by trailing his slip-covered fingers across their surfaces. However, he has avoided using the same technique on platters, fearing that the more two-dimensional forms would cause his designs to become too pictorial. He recently solved this dilemma by cutting a slip-painted jar into slabs and then, with the help of an assistant, pulling the pieces into rectangular shapes.
Photograph by Gary Mortensen.

the rest of the forest. There was a pond near the center of the acreage, and a small meadow in the northeast quadrant. Leafy ferns, leatherwood bushes, and wild hepatica grew everywhere, and Bresnahan spotted chanterelle mushrooms and trillium in the shadows. Suddenly, Grunloh stopped walking and placed his hand on the trunk of an enormous maple. "This is my favorite tree," he said, catching Bresnahan's eye and holding it in his gaze. "I'll sell you this land if you promise to take care of my trees."

Teacup (Johanna kiln, Tanegashima chamber), 1998, kaolin with oak ash glaze, 4 in. high. Although Bresnahan prefers the plasticity of stoneware clay, he occasionally works with regional kaolins. For this cup, he achieved a rich caramel color by dipping it in an oak ash glaze and then placing it in a sagger in the first row of the Tanegashima chamber. During the firing, the intense heat of the kiln caused the glaze to run and streak in an unusual way.
Photograph by Gary Mortensen.

At the time, the Bresnahans were renting a house near Saint John's. After purchasing Grunloh's land with the Bresnahans, Dean closed his business in St. Paul and moved close by into Schellinger's guest cabin. For the next two years, the Bresnahans and Dean met frequently to talk about their hopes for the property. Eventually, they developed a master plan. They envisioned an artists' colony with houses not only for the Bresnahans and Dean, but for four or five other artists and their families. Another structure would serve as a gallery, so members of the colony could exhibit and sell their work.

Since they were determined to live off the land without harming it, they hired a forester to survey it. He created a map of the woods and made recommendations about which trees to cut and when, so the forest would remain healthy and regenerative. They planned organic gardens near the center of the property and talked of dredging and deepening the pond to make it suitable for fish farming. And Bresnahan continued to mill lumber with Schellinger and stockpile it for the day they would begin to build.

In December 1984, the Bresnahans and Dean hiked into the woods, pulling a child's sled loaded with chain saws behind them. Following the forester's advice, they intended to take down several stands of poplar that had gone into decline. The resulting open areas would eventually become sites for their houses. But when the first few trees they cut became entangled in the neighboring branches and hung there like some gigantic trap ready to crush them, they suddenly became aware of the enormity of the task and their own lack of experience. By nightfall, however, they had managed to bring down the trees and to fell several more. The result of all their effort was hardly noticeable in the thick forest, but they had begun, and they were ecstatic. They worked in the evenings and on weekends throughout the long winter. Eventually, along the ridge of the gorge, they also had cleared a swath that would become the road into their property.

In early 1985, the project suddenly took on a sense of urgency. The owner of the house the Bresnahans rented had served them with an eviction notice. They had been good tenants and paid their rent on time, but the neighbors had started complaining about their unconventional lifestyle. In their desire to be self-sufficient, the Bresnahans had converted the garage into a barn and were raising chickens, rabbits, and sheep. They also had a horse, a wedding gift from a friend. The Bresnahans knew they needed their own place, but their acreage was far from ready. So, with Colette pregnant with their first child, they gave the animals away and relocated to a small, run-down apartment near the university. A year-and-a-half later, after they had arranged for electricity and had a well drilled, they moved a used mobile home onto their property. Finally, despite their modest beginning, they were living on their own land.

With the help of family and friends, they built their first substantial structure the next summer—a wood shop. Over the next decade, this large 22- by 40-foot building would serve as the center for their construction projects. There, through the cold winter

Small bottle (Johanna kiln, front fire chamber), 1995, stoneware with natural ash glaze, 7 1/4 in. high. As part of his commitment to making wares for daily use, Bresnahan routinely produces small serving bottles based on the flasks the Japanese use for sake (rice wine). Ash from the firing settled on the shoulder of this bottle, then liquefied and ran down the body in a single dramatic drip.
Photograph by Gary Mortensen.

Small bottle (Johanna kiln, Tanegashima chamber), 1997, stoneware with natural ash glaze, 6¼ in. high. When loading the kiln, Bresnahan often places small bottles and cups between larger jars and sculptures. During the firing, the unglazed surface of this humble bottle blushed to a deep aubergine while also receiving a heavy deposit of ash glaze in glassy greens.
Photograph by Gary Mortensen.

months, they milled and planed lumber and built trusses in preparation for fair-weather building. Framing the wood shop, however, was revelatory for Bresnahan, who had long assumed they would erect post-and-lintel structures on the property, like the farmhouses he had seen in Japan. Although they did make the shop in the Japanese style, lifting the 40-foot beams onto ten-foot posts had proved difficult and dangerous, especially since they lacked the pulley systems typically used in Japan. To ensure everyone's safety, Bresnahan and Dean decided to employ Western methods for future structures.

Shortly after the wood shop had been completed, Bresnahan's parents, who still lived in North Dakota, retired and expressed a desire to relocate to be closer to their children and grandchildren. Deeply influenced by Japanese practices, where extended families are common and elders are respected and valued, Bresnahan invited them to move permanently onto the land.

Still reeling from the hardships of building the wood shop, Bresnahan hired a local contractor to carry out Dean's design for his parents' house. During the summer of 1987, Bresnahan worked alongside Paul Koshoil and his crew, learning a variety of construction techniques. He helped build the forms for the concrete footings. He framed walls, built and hoisted roof trusses, and then prepared walls for stucco. Along with his brother Chad, friends, and a few apprentices,

Because summertime logging would damage the fragile forest floor, including rare wild orchids that grow everywhere on the Bresnahans' land, all logging there takes place during the winter. Here, a group of volunteers heads out into the woods, passing stacks of milled lumber on the right. Photograph by James R. Dean, January 1988.

he milled and installed tongue-and-groove floors in the house's interior and board-and-batten siding on the exterior. By late fall, Bresnahan's mother and father moved into the first house on the property.

Two years later, the Bresnahans were ready to begin work on their own home. During the interim, Bresnahan had milled thousands of boards for the construction and, at every opportunity, had gathered discarded materials that he hoped to put to good use. His comrade-in-arms in this quest was Brother William Borgerding, who had been a herdsman at Saint John's. After the dairy closed in 1958, Brother "Willie" worked in the monastery's wood shop and became a security guard. Walking from building to building at night making sure all was well had earned him the affectionate nickname of "Night Abbot." If Brother Willie found cast-off materials during his

Teapot (Johanna kiln, Tanegashima chamber), 2000, stoneware, 6 1/2 in. high. Reed handle by Paul Krueger. Works from the third, or Tanegashima, chamber of Bresnahan's kiln have soft surface textures and a variety of earth colors, like the fiery orange of this teapot. Photograph by Gary Mortensen.

Tea bowl (Johanna kiln, glaze chamber), 1997, stoneware with iron painting under a navy-bean straw ash glaze, 4 in. high, 4 9/16 in. diameter. Bresnahan created the pattern of mountain peaks on this tea bowl with his fingers: by tightly gripping the body of the vessel while dipping it in glaze. The unglazed areas also reveal a swath of purplish brown—evidence that Bresnahan brushed the bowl's surface with iron before glazing it.
Photograph by Gary Mortensen.

nocturnal forays that he believed could be reused, he would carry them back to the monastic garage or wood shed. He also gathered cardboard boxes and paper for Bresnahan, who used them as shipping materials for his ceramics.

One day, Brother Willie rushed into Bresnahan's studio with tears in his eyes. A portion of the wood shed was going to be converted into a storage place for housekeeping supplies, and his "collection" was slated to be thrown away. The very next day, Bresnahan hauled away 32 French doors, some with hand-carved decorations, which had once been in buildings in the monastery's original quadrangle. Thereafter, Bresnahan regularly went "dumpster diving" with the Night Abbot. When the university remodeled St. Thomas Aquinas Hall in 1986, they

salvaged light fixtures. When the monastery planned to bury thousands of old clay tiles it no longer wanted to save, they took them to build retaining walls. As they reached the bottom of the pile, they also discovered broken sheets of peach Byzantine marble, which had once lined the monks' shower stalls and, like the tiles, had been consigned to oblivion.

Other building materials came from elsewhere. To commemorate their first wedding anniversary, the Bresnahans visited a quarry in Jasper, Minnesota. There, they purchased irregular "end cuts" of pink quartzite at a deep discount. And their ever-resourceful friend Francis Schellinger supplied them with broken telephone poles, which had been discarded by the local power company but still could be milled into usable lumber.

Many people helped the Bresnahans build their house in 1989. Here, contractor Paul Koshoil and his construction crew join Bresnahan's family and friends to hoist roof trusses into place.
Photograph by James R. Dean, April 1989.

The House

Like his pottery, the house Bresnahan built combines Japanese aesthetics with American ingenuity. For James Dean, the challenge was to create a structure that would accommodate the family's lifestyle while still integrating elements of traditional Japanese design. Together, the Bresnahans and Dean poured over books about Japanese architecture and photographs of the Nakazato house and studio in Karatsu, choosing features they hoped to include in their own building. At the same time, they realized that Minnesota's severe winters, together with Bresnahan's desire to use recycled materials, would impact Dean's design and the ultimate look and function of the house. Nevertheless, they remained steadfast in their commitment to making a structure that would not only serve the family's needs but be energy efficient and aesthetically suitable for the site.

Bresnahan troweling stucco onto an exterior wall of the wood shop, the first building constructed on the property.
Photograph by James R. Dean, August 1988.

They began by positioning the two-story building on the crest of a ridge between two gorges. They left the forest to the north and east of the house untouched, to act as a natural barrier against winter's frigid winds. To the south, they selectively thinned out trees, to enable that side of the structure to be bathed in sunlight and to take advantage of a stunning view of the woods. They coated the upper surfaces of the exterior with stucco (mixed with wild rice hulls for color and texture) and covered the lower half with unpainted poplar siding. They also left the eaves and moldings unfinished, having read in a building manual published by the Army Corps of Engineers that unpainted poplar would last up to 125 years. Moreover, they liked the idea that the wood would weather to a silver gray and thus allow the building to blend into its natural surroundings.

To reflect the Bresnahans' belief in family and community, Dean designed three relatively large gathering areas: the main room, the library, and the kitchen. Bedrooms, seen primarily as spaces for sleeping, were intentionally kept simple and small, without the large closets, private bathrooms, and sitting areas so common in new American construction. (Initially, there were only two bedrooms, but recently, the Bresnahans converted an archival storage room into a third bedroom to meet the growing needs of their three children.)

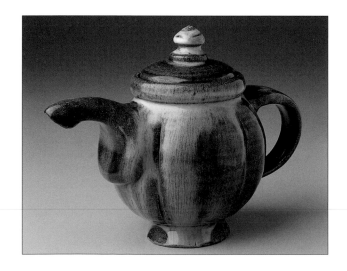

Melon-shaped teapot (Johanna kiln, glaze chamber), 1998, stoneware with a navy-bean straw ash glaze, 6 3/4 in. high.
Photograph by Gary Mortensen.

Bresnahan's younger brother Chad spent summer vacations working at the studio and helped construct the Takigama and Johanna kilns. Over the years, Chad also assisted with numerous projects on Bresnahan's property, from felling trees and milling lumber to framing buildings.
Photograph by Mark Strand, 1981.

From the beginning, the architecture was intended to bring the family together, rather than encouraging individuals to sequester themselves in private, self-sufficient domains. The importance of mealtime gatherings, especially, made the inclusion of an open hearth (*irori*) in the main room a top priority. In traditional Japanese farmhouses, household members routinely gather around the *irori* for warmth. While the Bresnahans' house has central heating, the *irori* functions as the same spiritual center for the family. But while Japanese hearths are at floor level, the Bresnahans knew that Americans—themselves included—would not be comfortable sitting on bent knees. Because of this, Dean elevated the entire living area, making it a raised platform with a sunken *irori* in the center. In this way, people can sit on the edge of the platform around the hearth with their feet still touching the floor.

Borrowing from Japanese aesthetics, the main room of the Bresnahans' house has an open hearth, post-and-lintel construction, clay walls, and sliding *shoji* screens.
Photograph by James R. Dean, July 2000.

Bresnahan finished the walls of a small bathroom with salvaged pieces of peach Byzantine marble, shown here with wooden shims before grouting. He laid the floor with white slip-painted tiles he made himself.

Photograph by James R. Dean, September 1989.

More than any other space in the house, the main room borrows most heavily from Japanese aesthetics and design. It has massive wooden posts and beams—connected by joinery Bresnahan learned to make while living in Japan. Two sides of the room are enclosed by *shoji*, sliding doors with translucent paper panels. The walls are finished with a fine layer of natural clay mixed with wild rice hulls. The west wall even includes a *tokonoma*, an alcove for the display of flowers or art. The prevalence of natural materials—clay, stone, and wood—without the applied embellishments typically found in American homes, like printed wallpapers, painted surfaces, and decorative moldings, gives the room an unaffected but sophisticated simplicity. Uncluttered by furniture, the space is light and airy, with family and guests using thin pillows or straw mats to sit on. The south side—a sweeping expanse of windows and sliding glass doors—opens up to spectacular views and lets out onto a wide stone terrace that cascades down into the surrounding landscape.

The main entryway and the bath also clearly reflect traditional Japanese customs. The entrance consists of a vestibule at ground level, where visitors remove their shoes before stepping up to the main floor. The comfort and informality of going shoeless appealed to the Bresnahans, as did the idea of leaving dirt-encrusted shoes at the door. Not only did the practice make for a cleaner interior but prevented grit from being tracked inside that could scratch and abrade the floors.

During his time in Japan, Bresnahan also developed an abiding affection for Japanese-style bathing. Finding American tubs too shallow, he hired a metalworker in nearby St. Joseph to fabricate a 92-gallon stainless-steel tub deep enough to allow bathers to easily submerge themselves up to their necks. Bresnahan covered the walls and floor of the room with tiles he made and outfitted the space with a shower and floor drain to enable the bather to wash completely before climbing into the steaming tub.

Other elements of the house's design reveal Bresnahan's commitment to energy efficiency. The embankment of glass on the south side captures solar energy during the long winter months, funneling it to the inside. Whereas in summer, deep overhanging eaves help shade the interior, protecting it from the sun's scorching rays. The building itself is heated entirely by a wood-burning boiler, which pumps hot water through flexible tubing in the concrete subfloor. Once warmed, the slab provides radiant heat for hours, unlike traditional furnaces that heat the air, which quickly dissipates once the furnace shuts off. But to efficiently distribute heat with an in-floor system, noninsulating materials need to be placed on the surface. The Japanese typically use wood and tatami, but such substances would have prevented the heat from escaping the concrete and warming the air. However, stone and tile conduct heat readily. So the Bresnahans used the peach Byzantine marble they had salvaged from Saint John's in the kitchen, white marble "end cuts" they had obtained in Cold Spring, Minnesota, in the library, and the pink quartzite they had purchased on their first wedding anniversary in the main room and entryway.

Other unusual features in the house also came about by making inventive use of an assortment of castoffs. Quartersawn oak panels, originally wainscoting in the monks' refectory at Saint John's, became doors for built-in cabinets in the Bresnahans' library. Two ornately carved capitals from the old abbey's baldachin became the finishing touches on two wooden columns that frame a small reading nook at the end of the room. And some of the 32 French doors that Bresnahan and Brother Willie had rescued years earlier became floor-to-ceiling cupboard doors in the kitchen and the adjoining hallway that leads to the back door.

Of course, none of this would have been possible without the assistance of many friends and relatives. The selfless support of so many people is especially remarkable given the strenuous nature of the work involved. In fact, in describing the effort needed to clear the land and construct the buildings, Mark Strand has jokingly dubbed the Bresnahans' property "the Gulag," after the Soviet Union's brutal labor camps. That so

In describing the effort involved in felling trees, photographer Mark Strand has jokingly dubbed the Bresnahans' property "the Gulag," after the Soviet Union's brutal labor camps. Here, Bresnahan (front), apprentice Stephen Earp, and Bresnahan's younger brother Chad (back) haul logs.
Photograph by James R. Dean, April 1988.

Tall bottles (Johanna kiln, front fire chamber), 1997, stoneware with natural ash glaze, 13 in. high (left), 10 1/2 in. high (right).
Photograph by Gary Mortensen.

In all of his endeavors, Bresnahan has also had the tireless support of his truest friend of all—his wife. As a licensed registered nurse, Colette has been able to see the family through financially from the very beginning, providing a steady source of income unlike the erratic earnings of her artist-husband. With considerable poise and grace, she trusted in both Bresnahan's artistic vision and James Dean's technical finesse to translate those dreams into reality. And with her uncommon ability to see something positive in nearly every situation, she has reveled in every stage of the process, including the day her five-year-old son "helped" build the framework under the living-room floor. Recalling his too-numerous and somewhat crooked nails, she lovingly says, "Such memories make the house my home."

After working days as a registered nurse, Colette Bresnahan helps her husband plane lumber at night.
Photograph by James R. Dean, March 1990.

many individuals have willingly journeyed to central Minnesota to help, even in wintertime and from long distances, is partly explained by computer-software designer Carl Philabaum. "For people who spend their days doing such mental tasks as reading, analyzing, writing, and working with computers," he theorizes, "helping Bresnahan build a house or fire his kiln brings them back to something more elemental and physical."

Cups (Johanna kiln, glaze chamber), 1997, stoneware with iron painting under a navy-bean straw ash glaze, 4 3/8 in. high. Japanese Karatsu ware often features simplified and rapidly painted motifs from nature. After returning to the United States, Bresnahan started making his own painted wares using images from his Midwestern surroundings. These cups show migrating birds in flight.
Photograph by Gary Mortensen.

Spice jar (Johanna kiln, front fire chamber), 1997, stoneware with natural ash glaze, 3 7/8 in. high. As a way to keep himself challenged, Bresnahan adds new forms to his repertoire every year. Over time, he has created a variety of small jars for storing spices and other condiments. A natural ash glaze dramatically adorns the undulating profile of this example. Photograph by Gary Mortensen.

Sculptor Paul Krueger has woven reed and vine handles for Bresnahan's teapots for many years. Here, he makes a *jizaikake* (an adjustable hanger for suspending an iron kettle or cooking pot over a hearth) for the Bresnahans' house. Photograph by James R. Dean, August 1995.

Bresnahan and filmmaker John Whitehead (right) in North Dakota near a mound of flax-straw ash on the Leo Mock farm. In 1997, Whitehead directed and produced *Clay, Wood, Fire, Spirit: The Pottery of Richard Bresnahan*—a documentary film for Minnesota Public Television. The program aired nationally in 1998 and won two Emmy awards. Photograph by Todd Hunter Strand, October 1996.

A typical gathering at the Bresnahans' takes place around the *irori*. For this meal, the family was joined by musician Lauden Wainwright III (across from Bresnahan), photographer Lee Hanley, musician John McCutcheon, textile artist Joyce Crain, and computer-software designer Carl Philabaum, among others.
Photograph by James R. Dean, April 1991.

Kindred Spirits

"Many artists leave the Midwest and move to New York or L.A. to shun their rural background," says Stewart Turnquist, coordinator of the Minnesota Artists Exhibition Program at The Minneapolis Institute of Arts. "But Richard chose to come back here, to create a center, and to promote the very earth of the place as an asset." In truth, Bresnahan is the antithesis of the misanthropic artist who rejects society and finds comfort in self-imposed exile. And his house, although remote, is the furthest thing imaginable from a hermit's hideaway. On any given evening, he invites

at least one guest to join him and his family for dinner, and with surprising frequency, the Bresnahans set two or three extra places at the *irori*. In fact, some apprentices eat with them so often they act like part of the family, helping to cook, to carry food to the table, and to clean up afterward. And usually once a week, Colette hosts a dinner she "worries about"— that requires special planning and preparation for someone with whom they are on less familiar terms or whose status commands greater attention.

"Somebody wrote a book a few years ago asserting that the greatest number of people possible in a single person's social sphere is 150—usually less," notes Patrick Herson, a physician in New Hampshire,

Bresnahan first met sculptor Kaneko Jun (left) in Karatsu during the summer of 1976. After teaching at the Rhode Island School of Design, Kaneko had returned to Japan and was building his own house and studio in Nagura. He now lives in Omaha, Nebraska, and visits Bresnahan in Minnesota.
Photograph by James R. Dean, May 1982.

who has been visiting the pottery and the Bresnahans for several years. "Richard is the exception." Given Bresnahan's 25-year career, it is not surprising that his circle of colleagues is far-reaching and international in scope. Japanese potter and painter Kakutani Mitsuo of Earlham College in Richmond, Indiana,

Artist Chuck Hindes teaches ceramics at the University of Iowa. He first met Bresnahan in 1980, when he went to Saint John's with sculptor Kaneko Jun. Every year since then, Hindes has taken his students to Collegeville to help fire Bresnahan's kiln.

Photograph by James R. Dean, June 1997.

whom Bresnahan first met abroad in 1976, visited the studio frequently during the first decade of its existence and has participated in every firing of the Johanna kiln since 1995. Likewise, American ceramist Chuck Hindes, a professor at the University of Iowa in Iowa City, makes the 350-mile drive to Collegeville every year with his students to attend the fall firing. Many past apprentices and visiting artists also stay in touch, including Kevin Flicker, who teaches ceramics at the University of Minnesota in Morris, and David Swenson, who teaches at North Dakota State University in Fargo. Like colleagues in any field, they exchange information, swap stories, and find satisfaction in their shared experiences.

But the Bresnahans have made their home more than a haven for fellow potters. An astounding array of people from vastly different disciplines find their way to the house in the woods—and return again and again. Part of the enchantment comes from the house itself, which exudes an aura of serenity and is adorned with sculptures, paintings, and photographs, as well as ceramics. As compelling is Bresnahan's remarkable ability to make everybody feel significant and uniquely valued. He accomplishes this in a multitude of ways: in his quickness to offer a cup of tea, to ask about family members (with an astounding memory for names), to seek advice and listen to the response, to proffer small gifts of pottery, and to unfailingly give thanks. At a 1996 opening to an exhibition of Bresnahan's work at The Minneapolis Institute of Arts, Director Evan Maurer humorously observed that everyone present—all 330 attendees— felt that they were Bresnahan's very best friend.

For many, a visit to the Saint John's Pottery represents a chance to be with the community that has grown up around the Bresnahans—especially during the studio's annual firings and Bresnahan's Fourth-of-July birthday party. For some, these events function as an antidote to the increasing isolation of modern life, where television, computers, and cell phones have all but supplanted the need for direct human contact. For photographer Mark Strand, these affairs recall the family reunions and Sunday get-togethers that were a regular part of his North Dakota upbringing. For Patrick Herson, who meets patients one-by-one in a strictly prescribed manner, these happenings offer a unique opportunity to be part of a larger family of sorts, which even values the youngest members of the group. "I brought my three-year-old daughter with me to watch the unloading of the kiln, and the assistants started handing her cups to carry to the truck. I was nervous that she would drop one," he recalls. "But Richard pulled me aside and told me not to worry—that she wasn't going to break anything on purpose, and that nothing is as valuable as the experience of a child."

To an extent, it is the Bresnahans' remarkable ability to inspire by their own example that draws people to them. "Most people are mired in self-doubt," says Carl Philabaum, who has known the Bresnahans for twenty years. "There aren't many people who have the confidence to forgo security, risk failure, and endure great hardships to pursue their dreams. But they did it." Dentist Daniel Estrem echoes those sentiments, "I have a profession, and then I practice my art—classical guitar—on the side. It is heartening to see someone doing it all the way."

In fact, after twenty-five years, the Bresnahans still have an unwavering enthusiasm for their chosen professions. Within minutes of entering the Saint John's studio, a visitor is likely to see Bresnahan holding up a cup or plate and exclaiming with wide-eyed wonder, "Look at these colors! This was a tremendous firing!" And while Colette is more reserved than her gregarious husband, she speaks with equal intensity about nursing and the plight of the sick and the aging—from the ravages of Alzheimer's to the labyrinthine procedures of medical insurance companies, all topics she is acutely aware of in her position as a senior registered nurse at the veterans hospital in St. Cloud, Minnesota.

Given today's penchant for hype and disingenuous self-promotion, it seems all the more admirable that the Bresnahans actually practice what they preach. They express their concern for the environment by living in an energy-efficient house that is heated by wood—a renewable resource. They demonstrate their misgivings about chemical additives by buying organic foods and cultivating their own fruits and vegetables. They reject America's rampant consumerism by severely limiting their family's exposure to television and by shopping at locally owned businesses instead of megamalls and superstores. And they repudiate the trend toward anti-intellectualism by filling their house with books and by having meaningful conversations at their dinner table. As textile artist Joyce Crain says, "There's not much chitchat that goes on at the Bresnahans', but there's exhilarating talk about big ideas and issues." In this way, the Bresnahans embody the "monastic" ideal advocated by social critic Morris Berman, who sees the preservation and ultimate resurgence of American culture as something that rests with the individual, for whom craftsmanship, scholarship, and social and environmental responsibility are more important than wealth, power, and fame (Berman, *The Twilight of American Culture*, p. 157).

Foliate bowl (Johanna kiln, glaze chamber), 1997, stoneware with a navy-bean straw ash glaze, 6 7/8 in. high, 10 7/8 in. diameter.
Photograph by Gary Mortensen.

Home Fires

Despite the somewhat rarefied atmosphere of the Bresnahan household, there is also much that is ordinary. They grapple with the same challenges that confront other families with school-age children, including hectic schedules that are complicated by numerous school activities and sporting events. Like all homeowners, they struggle to find time for odd jobs and routine maintenance. And they juggle work with vacation plans to eke out occasional holidays and visits to faraway family members and friends.

With the Saint John's studio and ceramics program now firmly established, Bresnahan continues to plan for the future. Over the past two years, he and Colette have been designing a small home studio with the help of James Dean. Ground-breaking for the structure, which is adjacent to the house, occurred in March 2001. The project grew out of Bresnahan's simple desire to return to his potter's wheel late in the evening after spending time with his family.

After years of contending with Minnesota's winter weather and icy roads, he has become increasingly reluctant to make the ten-mile drive back to Saint John's late at night. A small studio at home, he reasoned, would solve this dilemma and also provide him with private time to work. And since the Saint John's studio has become the thriving center of activity he intended it to be, Bresnahan wants to give his advanced apprentices the opportunity to create without always having their mentor close at hand. As the concept for the home studio has

The Bresnahans have always encouraged their children to help with the vegetable gardens. Here, Margaret Adelaide and Richard III take part in the spring planting, while their mother offers gentle guidance.
Photograph by James R. Dean, May 1989.

evolved, it also will include a loft for Colette. With their youngest child now in school, Colette wants to approach gardening in a more systematic manner: keeping detailed annual records and storing seeds from successful plantings for future use. In addition, she hopes to raise sheep again and needs a place to process and spin her own wool.

Large jar **(Johanna kiln, front fire chamber), 1995, stoneware with white porcelain slip, iron painting, and natural ash glaze, 28 1/2 in. high.**
Photograph by Gary Mortensen.

Opposite page: Richard Bresnahan.
Photograph by James R. Dean, 1996.

Finally, the Bresnahans hope the small studio will have a positive influence on their own children as well. While their son and two daughters go to the Saint John's studio nearly every day after school, it is usually just a convenient meeting place before the ride home. A studio at the house would not only allow the children to spend time with their parents but encourage them to explore artistic avenues of their own.

Since 1983, when the Bresnahans and James Dean bought Rudy Grunloh's land, not everything has gone according to the master plan. Dean's own house, on the west side of the property near the original tree house, did not get built until 1993. And the idea of four or more additional homesteads with an artists' colony and a gallery somehow never materialized. "Having a plan is not so much about achieving a goal," says Dean. "It's about having an ideal and a philosophy about how you will conduct yourself in the process." In this regard, Richard Bresnahan—in remaining true to himself and his own beliefs—has conducted himself very well indeed.

Appendices

The Takigama Kiln

Bresnahan based the design for his first kiln at Saint John's on *noborigama* (climbing kilns) he had seen and helped to build during his apprenticeship in Japan with Nakazato Takashi. Named after Takashi's son Taki, the Takigama kiln was completed in the fall of 1979 and first fired that November. It remained in use until 1991. Measuring 41 feet from the front ash pit to the chimney's back wall, it consisted of a relatively small front fire chamber, three glaze chambers, and a Tanegashima chamber with three stoking portals plus a fourth in a side door.

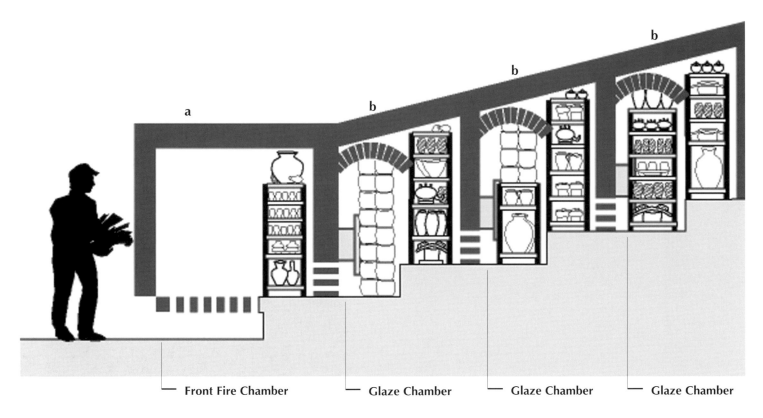

| Front Fire Chamber | Glaze Chamber | Glaze Chamber | Glaze Chamber |

a The front fire chamber had a single, centrally located stoking box. The shallowness of the chamber, a mere five feet, made the fire difficult to control. Flames tended to shoot directly through to the ground-level flues leading into the next chamber, overfiring works placed on the lower shelves in the first chamber and underfiring those on the upper shelves.

b The second, third, and fourth chambers of the Takigama kiln were reserved for glazed ware. While these chambers often produced successful wares, pots fired in the third and fourth chambers often lacked the rich textures and tonal variations associated with wood firing. Consequently, in designing the Johanna kiln, Bresnahan made a single, larger glaze chamber, which takes better advantage of the heat and ash generated by the adjoining front fire chamber.

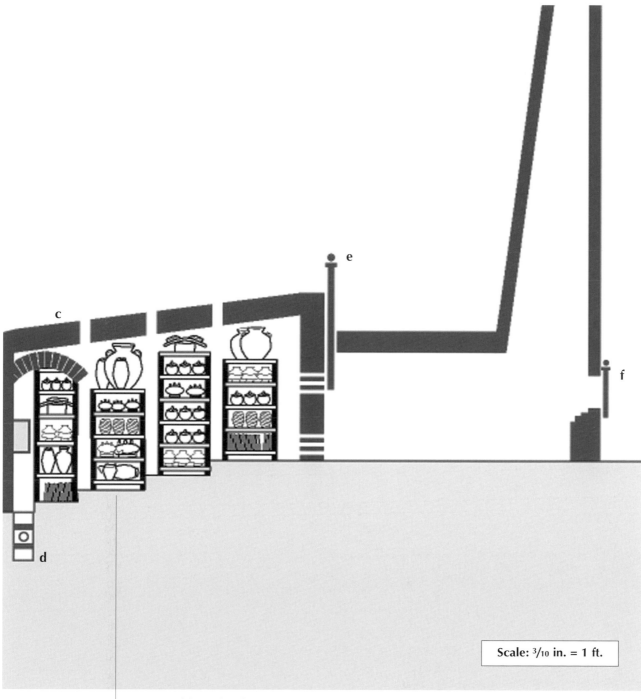

Tanegashima Chamber

c   Bresnahan reserved the ten-foot Tanegashima chamber for unglazed ware. However, the relative shortness of the chamber and difficulty in preventing backdrafts from the chimney during the cooling period minimized the subtle surface effects desired on works from this area of the kiln. Consequently, when Bresnahan designed the Johanna kiln, he greatly expanded the Tanegashima chamber and reconfigured the flue system.

d   A brick-lined channel with a water pipe above and an ash collection pit below enabled Bresnahan to introduce water into the Tanegashima chamber during firing.

e   A kaolinite M board attached to a pulley served as a mechanical damper.

f   An atmospheric plate damper.

The Johanna Kiln

Designed by Bresnahan and named in honor of his mentor, Sister Johanna Becker, the Johanna kiln was finished in October 1994, after two years of planning and construction. A massive *noborigama*, the 87-foot-long brick structure consists of a front fire chamber, a glaze chamber, a Tanegashima chamber with nine pairs of stoking portals, a long subterranean flue, and a chimney. With more than 1,600 cubic feet of interior space, it is the largest wood-burning kiln in North America and was first fired in October 1995. Because more pottery can be accommodated by its large interior, it is usually fired only once a year.

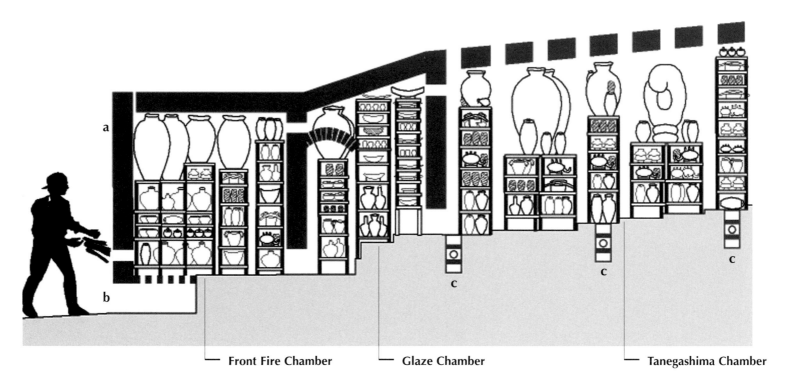

Front Fire Chamber   Glaze Chamber   Tanegashima Chamber

a   The front and back walls of the kiln include massive steel-framed concrete doors, which are suspended from wheels that run along an overhead I-beam. Pushed aside during loading and unloading, the doors facilitate the moving of large sculptural works into and out of the kiln.

b   Twin stoking boxes at the right and left corners of the front fire chamber help achieve even heat distribution throughout the first and second chambers.

c   Brick-lined channels with water pipes above and ash collection pits below allow Bresnahan to introduce water into the Tanegashima chamber during firing.

d   The 37-foot-long subterranean flue with portal dampers enables Bresnahan to create sufficient back pressure to slow the heat's movement throughout the entire kiln.

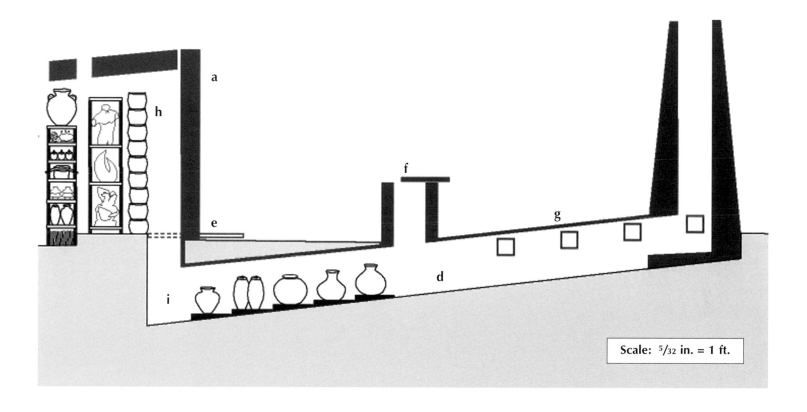

Scale: $^5/_{32}$ in. = 1 ft.

e   The mechanical dampering system consists of six bricks (24 x 12 x 3 in.), which were formed from a castable refractory material reinforced with stainless-steel pins. By sliding these bricks into various positions across the opening to the flue chamber, airflow can be controlled throughout the length of the kiln.

f   Two atmospheric plate dampers.

g   Atmospheric portal dampers (three on the flue chamber and two on the sides of the chimney).

h   Recently, Bresnahan has been placing wild rice hulls in a wall of saggers at the back of the Tanegashima chamber. During the prolonged firing, the hulls become reduced to a fine ash, which he uses for glazes.

i   After the fourth firing of the Johanna kiln in 1999, Bresnahan discovered that the bottom of the flue chamber had a heavy coating of natural ash glaze. Because temperatures in this area of the kiln can exceed 2,580° centigrade, the natural glazes that form there differ from those produced in the front fire chamber and tend toward clear browns and greens. To capitalize on this, Bresnahan has begun to place a few pots in the flue chamber during his firings, inserting them into the space from the Tanegashima chamber and positioning them on firebrick pads leveled in a castable refractory material.

Ten-Day Firing Schedule

This four-page chart plots the temperature fluctuations in each chamber of the Johanna kiln during a ten-day firing and a ten-day cooling period. The chart presents an average of temperature readings taken from five firings of the kiln since 1995. The chart also assumes fair weather conditions with relatively low humidity. The written information accompanying the chart describes the procedures used to achieve a successful wood firing.

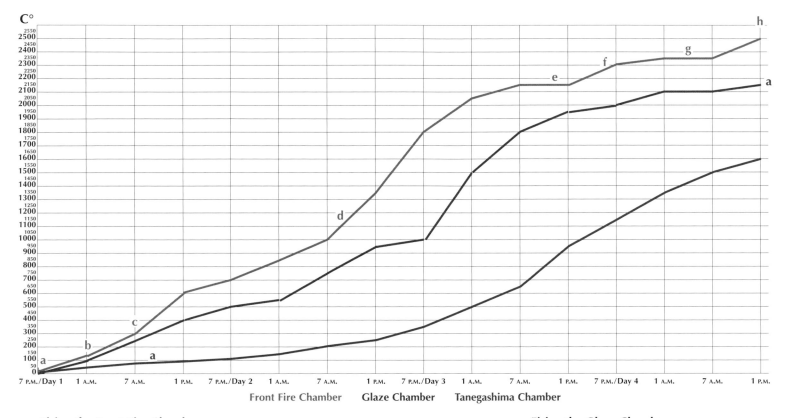

Front Fire Chamber   Glaze Chamber   Tanegashima Chamber

Firing the Front Fire Chamber

a Start fires in the ash pits, stoking both pits equally with dried wood, using mostly pine.

b The first shift change should occur. Beginning shifts last for six hours and involve two people.

c Slowly begin increasing the amount of wood and the frequency of stoking to about every 15 minutes. Atmospheric dampers should remain closed to speed the draft.

d When the front fire chamber reaches 1,050° to 1,190° centigrade, start stoking through the doors located above the ash pits with two wet 4-ft. logs about 6 inches in diameter. Re-stoke before the logs completely burn, usually every 30 to 40 minutes. At the same time, continue to stoke the ash pits.

e Increase the frequency of stoking through the doors with wet logs and wet split wood, using elm, cottonwood, willow, basswood, oak, and poplar. Open passive dampers in the chimney to slow the draft. Then stop stoking the ash pits.

f When cone 8 has fallen and fly ash is tacking onto the surface of the ceramics, lessen the amount of wood used but maintain the stoking rhythm.

g Fly ash will layer the works' surfaces as cones 9 through 12 fall and cone 13 begins to soften. Allow the temperature to drop 50° centigrade, from 2,320° to 2,270° centigrade for one to two hours before progressing from cone 9 to 10 and so on. After cone 10 has fallen, perform a draw test to assess the amount of fly-ash layering.

h Through the front doors, stoke the first chamber for the final time. Then close and seal that chamber. Maintain narrow air intake in both ash pits. Wait 10 to 15 minutes for the flame movement through the chamber to stop.

i When the front chamber cools to between 900° and 1,000° centigrade, begin stoking the ash pits again with scrap wood to maintain that temperature throughout the duration of the firing. This minimizes the temperature differential between the front and back of the kiln as successive chambers are fired, thus decreasing the stress on the kiln itself. It also prevents large works from cooling too quickly and cracking. Wares in the neighboring glaze chamber also benefit from prolonged exposure to mid-range temperatures, which allow the minerals in the ash glazes to continue to migrate, creating temmoku-like results.

Firing the Glaze Chamber

a After opening the side stoking door in the glaze chamber, begin cross-stoking. Place more wood toward the back wall and stoking door and less wood near the center to prevent overfiring works at the core of the chamber and underfiring those near the walls. Close the mechanical dampers until the flame rolls upward, toward the ceiling of the arch. Open all passive dampers (3 side holes, 2 chimney, and 2 top adjusters).

b When cone 12 has fallen in the first row, cone 10 in the second row, and cone 8 in the third row of the glaze chamber (after approximately eight hours of stoking followed by one hour of "maintenance" stoking to "soak" the works), close and seal the glaze chamber. Open the mechanical dampers and close the atmospheric dampers. Wait 15 minutes and begin stoking the third chamber.

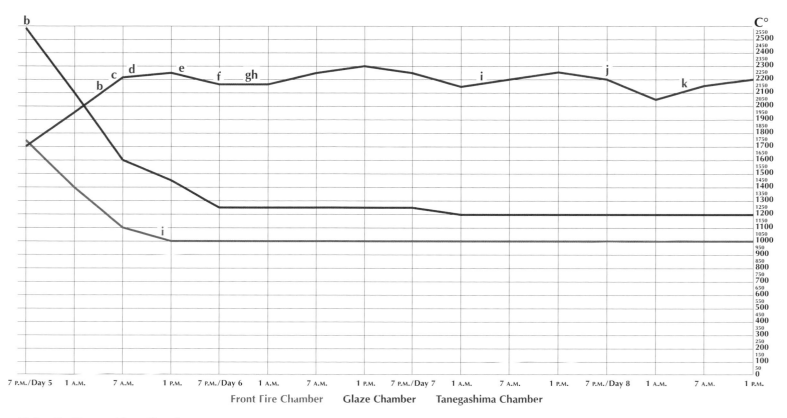

C°

	2550
	2500
	2450
	2400
	2350
	2300
	2250
	2200
	2150
	2100
	2050
	2000
	1950
	1900
	1850
	1800
	1750
	1700
	1650
	1600
	1550
	1500
	1450
	1400
	1350
	1300
	1250
	1200
	1150
	1100
	1050
	1000
	950
	900
	850
	800
	750
	700
	650
	600
	550
	500
	450
	400
	350
	300
	250
	200
	150
	100
	50
	0

7 P.M./Day 5   1 A.M.   7 A.M.   1 P.M.   7 P.M./Day 6   1 A.M.   7 A.M.   1 P.M.   7 P.M./Day 7   1 A.M.   7 A.M.   1 P.M.   7 P.M./Day 8   1 A.M.   7 A.M.   1 P.M.

Front Fire Chamber   Glaze Chamber   Tanegashima Chamber

Firing the Tanegashima Chamber

a Open five stoking windows in the Tanegashima chamber to accelerate the drying of the kiln and the pots. Only close the five Tanegashima stoking windows when a glass held over the chambers' windows does not fog up.

b Stoke the first set of windows of the Tanegashima chamber with wet wooden poles, approximately 7 ft. long, made of poplar, basswood, ironwood, or maple, using two or three poles per stoke. Adjust stoking rate to hold the temperature at cone 8 (2,240° centigrade) for five-and-a-half days. This will help achieve a broader clay palette and promote glazing tonalities that are different from those produced in the front fire chamber. Because stoking occurs every 30 minutes, four to five people are needed for each stoking shift.

c After about 13 hours of slow stoking, the first set of windows of the chamber will reach maturity at 2,240° centigrade. Before progressing to the third set of windows (skipping the second set because of pots and kiln furniture in that location), cones 1 and 2 must fall on the floor of the third stoking windows. Begin stoking the third set of windows with thin poles placed between the rows of

the kiln furniture to build a bed of charcoal. At the same time, continue to stoke the first set of windows.

d When cones 4 and 5 fall in the third set of windows and cones 1 and 2 have fallen on the floor of the fourth windows, begin stoking the fourth set of windows with thin poles. Continue to stoke windows 1 and 3 until a bed of charcoal is well established.

e When cones 4 and 5 fall in the fourth set of windows and cones 1 and 2 have fallen on the floor of the sixth windows, begin stoking the sixth set of windows (avoiding the fifth set of windows because of pots and kiln furniture in that location). Because of the distance between the fourth and sixth windows, the time required to reach cone 1 in the sixth windows will be much longer (approximately 14 hours).

f When cones 4 and 5 fall in the sixth windows and cone 1 has fallen on the floor of the seventh windows, begin stoking the seventh set of windows.

g When cones 4 and 5 fall in the seventh set of windows, begin stoking the eighth set of windows. This progression from the seventh to eighth windows can happen fairly

quickly—between four to seven hours. Cloudy or rainy weather can slow the maturation of the eighth set of windows. The average interval between stoking is 20 minutes during the day and 30 minutes at night.

h When the eighth set of windows matures to cone 2 and charcoal has built up to the windows, begin back-stoking windows 8, 7, 6, 4, and 3. Charcoal beneath these windows should be maintained at a depth of 6.5 ft. The space for stoking between the charcoal bed and the ceiling of the arch should not exceed 5.5 inches.

i Slowly pour one liter of water into each of the channels beneath the first set of windows and between windows 3 and 4, and 7 and 8. Begin stoking more frequently with less wood to raise the temperature. If the temperature drops below 1,950° centigrade and windows 6, 7, and 8 are very full with charcoal, stop stoking until the charcoal burns down to 12 or 18 inches below the windows, thereby increasing the air flow.

j Perform draw tests from windows 3 and 8 to check on the surface patterning, coloration, and amount of carbon on the vessels.

k Repeat i.

Firing Schedule *continued*

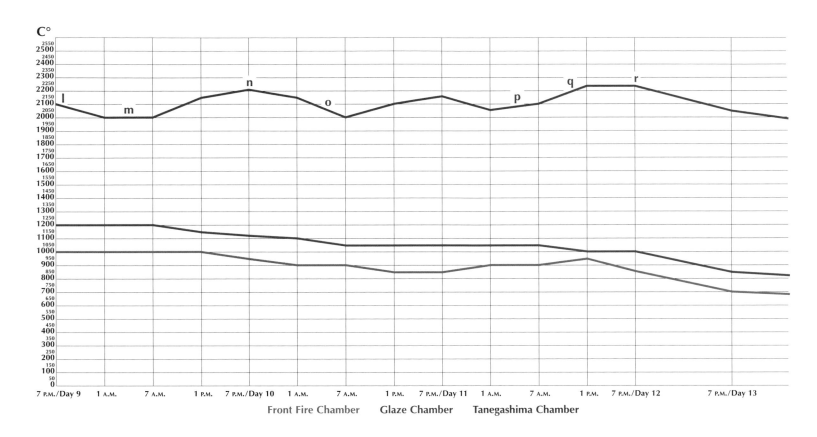

Front Fire Chamber   Glaze Chamber   Tanegashima Chamber

l Perform draw tests from windows 3 and 8 to check on the surface patterning, coloration, and amount of carbon on the vessels.

m Slowly pour one liter of water into each of the channels beneath the first set of windows and between windows 3 and 4, and 7 and 8. Begin stoking more frequently with less wood to raise the temperature. If the temperature drops below 1,950° centigrade and windows 6, 7, and 8 are very full with charcoal, stop stoking until the charcoal burns down to 12 or 18 inches below the windows, thereby increasing the air flow.

n Repeat l.

o Repeat m.

p Repeat m.

q Repeat l.

r For the final stoke, fill each window with wood. Then seal each window with a mixture of wet newspaper, clay, and sand. Pour clay slurry over the exterior roof arch to seal any cracks. This sealing process should not take longer than 30 minutes. After the flame is no longer visible in the flue tunnel, close and seal the front fire mouth with wet clay and shut the mechanical damper to prevent oxygen from back drafting into the Tanegashima chamber. The charcoal will burn slowly during the cooling process, keeping the interior atmosphere stable.

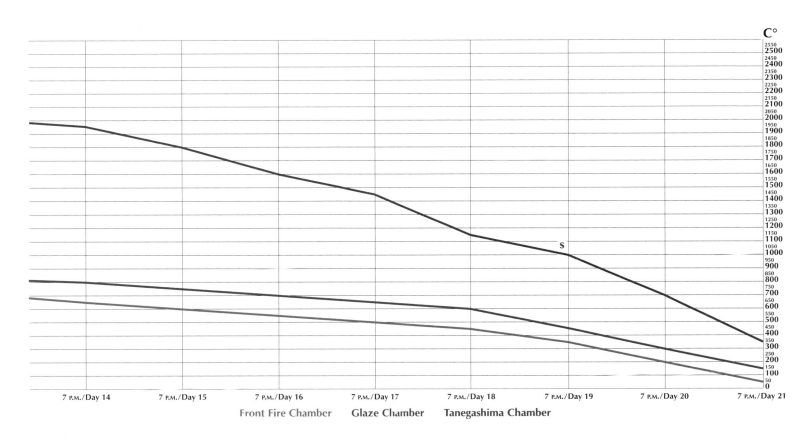

Front Fire Chamber   **Glaze Chamber**   **Tanegashima Chamber**

s Open the mechanical dampers and front ash pits about four inches to allow air to move rapidly through the kiln.

Opening and Unloading the Kiln

It takes about ten days for the kiln to cool down. Opening the kiln starts 20 days after the firing began with the coolest chamber—the front fire chamber. After the first chamber is emptied, the glaze chamber is opened and unloaded—a process that usually occurs 22 days after the firing was initiated. Two days later, the Tanegashima chamber is opened. Since it was the last chamber to be fired, it is the last to cool, and therefore the last to be unloaded.

Signature and Seals

Bresnahan signs his works with an uppercase R, the first initial of Richard, his given name. He then places a single dot below the R to signify that he represents the first generation in his family to be a potter.

Bresnahan based his original studio seal on the altar, cross, and baldachin in Saint John's second abbey church, which was designed by Marcel Breuer.

After finishing his second kiln at Saint John's in 1994, the Johanna kiln, Bresnahan has created a different seal for each firing, making use of a triangle, a symbol for stability. Works from the kiln's first firing, which occurred in October 1995, carry an impression composed of two dots enclosed in a triangle. The two dots stand for Bresnahan and his wife, Colette, whereas the three sides of the triangle refer to their three children.

This seal appears on works from the second firing (May 1997) of the Johanna kiln.

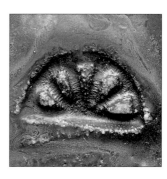

In conjunction with an exhibition of his works at The Minneapolis Institute of Arts in 1996, Bresnahan conducted a series of workshops at the museum. He impressed the pottery he made during these demonstrations with a rose, which symbolizes Villa Rosa, the ten-acre estate on which the Institute was built. Bresnahan fired the works bearing this seal in May 1997 in the Johanna kiln.

This seal identifies works from the third firing (September 1998) of the Johanna kiln.

This seal can be found on works from the fourth firing (October 1999) of the Johanna kiln.

This seal appears on works from the fifth firing (October 2000) of the Johanna kiln.

Exhibition History and Collections

Solo Exhibitions

1980

Benedicta Arts Center Gallery, College of Saint Benedict, St. Joseph, Minnesota

Alcuin Library, Saint John's University, Collegeville, Minnesota

1981

Plains Art Museum, Fargo, North Dakota

1982

The Society of Arts and Crafts, Boston, Massachusetts

Rourke Art Gallery, Moorhead, Minnesota

1984

Owatonna Arts Council, Owatonna, Minnesota

Benedicta Arts Center Gallery, College of Saint Benedict, St. Joseph, Minnesota

1986

Nobles County Art Center, Worthington, Minnesota

1987

Stearns County Historical Society, St. Cloud, Minnesota

The Society of Arts and Crafts, Boston, Massachusetts

1989

The University of Minnesota, Morris, Minnesota

1990

St. Paul Gallery, St. Paul, Minnesota

1996

The Minneapolis Institute of Arts, Minneapolis, Minnesota

1997

Rehfeld's Dakota Galleries, Sioux Falls, South Dakota

The Howard Conn Fine Arts Gallery, Minneapolis, Minnesota

1998

Minnesota Historical Society, St. Paul, Minnesota

Red Lake Falls Clayworks, Red Lake Falls, Minnesota

1999

Red Lake Falls Clayworks, Red Lake Falls, Minnesota

Group Exhibitions

1980–97

Annual Midwestern Invitational Exhibition, Moorhead, Minnesota

1981

Metro Center Museum, Rockford, Illinois

Pittsburgh Center for the Arts, Pittsburgh, Pennsylvania

1983

Kiehle Visual Arts Gallery, St. Cloud State University, St. Cloud, Minnesota

1984

Lill Street Gallery, Chicago, Illinois

North Dakota Museum of Art, Grand Forks, North Dakota

Southern Illinois University, Edwardsville, Illinois

Esther Saks Gallery, Chicago, Illinois

Benedicta Arts Center, College of Saint Benedict, St. Joseph, Minnesota

1985

Southern Illinois University, Edwardsville, Illinois

1986

Rourke Art Gallery, Moorhead, Minnesota

C. G. Rein Galleries, Edina, Minnesota

1991

University of Iowa Museum of Art, Iowa City, Iowa

1997

North Dakota State University, Fargo, North Dakota

Gustavus Adolphus College, St. Peter, Minnesota

Edina Arts Center, Edina, Minnesota

Memorial Union Gallery, North Dakota State University, Fargo, North Dakota

1998

University of Wisconsin, La Crosse, Wisconsin

1999

International Organization of Woodfire Artists, University of Iowa Museum of Art, Iowa City, Iowa

Woodard Gallery, Iowa City, Iowa

2001

The Goldstein Museum of Design, University of Minnesota, St. Paul, Minnesota

General Mills Gallery, Minneapolis, Minnesota

Collections

Mary Griggs Burke Collection, New York, New York

Edina Art Center, Edina, Minnesota

The Goldstein Museum of Design, University of Minnesota, St. Paul, Minnesota

Hill Reference Library, St. Paul, Minnesota

Idemitsu Museum of Art, Tokyo, Japan

Sarah and David Lieberman Collection, Phoenix, Arizona

Earl Millard Collection, St. Louis, Missouri

The Minneapolis Institute of Arts, Minneapolis, Minnesota

Minnesota Historical Society, St. Paul, Minnesota

Nagasaki Holocaust Museum, Nagasaki, Japan

Nobles County Art Center, Worthington, Minnesota

North Dakota State University, Grand Forks, North Dakota

Owatonna Art Center, Owatonna, Minnesota

Plains Art Museum, Fargo, North Dakota

Kimiko and John Powers Collection, Carbondale, Colorado

Rourke Art Gallery, Moorhead, Minnesota

Yamanouchi Tea Ceremony Foundation, Kyoto, Japan

Apprentices and Visiting Artists

Richard Bresnahan began accepting apprentices soon after his arrival at Saint John's University in 1979. Since he considers his studio and kiln to be community resources, he also encourages established artists from other disciplines to apply for short-term residencies. Many of the following apprentices and visiting artists had financial support from two Minnesota foundations: the Grotto and the Jerome. A + indicates individuals who were awarded grants from the Grotto Foundation, whereas a * represents those who received funds from the Jerome Foundation.

Apprentices

Douglas Smith, Summer 1979–Spring 1980, Landscape Architect, Inverness, California

Alan Peirson, Summer 1979–Spring 1980, Potter and Sculptor, Calistoga, California

Tim Smith, Fall 1980–Spring 1981, Sculptor and Potter; Instructor, Cypress Lake Center for the Arts High School, Fort Myers, Florida

+ Charles Matthews, Fall 1982–Fall 1983, Potter, Washburn, Wisconsin

+ Karen Kaeter, Fall 1982–Spring 1983, Occupational Therapist, San Francisco, California

+ Father Daniel Lenz, Fall 1984–Spring 1985, Sculptor; Ceramics Instructor, Mount Michael High School, Mount Michael Abbey, Elkhorn, Nebraska

+ David Swenson, Fall 1984–Spring 1985, Sculptor; Assistant Professor, North Dakota State University, Fargo, North Dakota

+ Kevin Flicker, Summer 1985, Potter; Teaching Specialist, University of Minnesota, Morris, Minnesota

+ Kimm Pruit, Fall 1985–Spring 1986, Sculptor, Chicago, Illinois

+ Kevin Brown, Spring 1986, Teacher, Duluth, Minnesota

+ Stephen Earp, March 1987–November 1988, Potter, Old Sturbridge Village, Sturbridge, Massachusetts

+ Paul Wegner, Spring 1989, Photographer and Potter, Burlingame, California

+ Eric Anderson, Summer 1990–Spring 1991, Artist and Potter, Stevens Point, Wisconsin

+ Grant Herzog, Fall 1990–Summer 1992, Construction Contractor, Fargo, North Dakota

+ James LaChance, Summer–Fall 1993, Sculptor, St. Paul, Minnesota

+ Gabriel Stockinger, Summer 1994–Summer 1995, Chef, St. Paul, Minnesota

+ Christopher Douglas, Spring 1996–Summer 1996, Photographer and Potter, Grand Forks, North Dakota

+ Daniel Siverson, Spring 1996–Fall 1998, Sculptor, Bemidji, Minnesota

+ Samuel Johnson, Summer 1996–Fall 1999, Potter, Copenhagen, Denmark

+ Katherine Mathieson, Fall 1996–Fall 1997, Bookbinder and Restorer, Portland, Maine

+ Matthew Cartier, Summer 1997–Fall 1998, Potter, Minneapolis, Minnesota

+ Catherine Braun, Spring–Summer 1999, K–12 Art Teacher, Burnsville, Minnesota

+ Debra Hulbert, Summer 1999, Student and Potter, Buffalo, Minnesota

+ Jennifer Otis, Summer–Fall 1999, Potter; Adjunct Faculty, Mount Mercy College, Cedar Rapids, Iowa

+ Michael Carlson, Summer 1999–Fall 2000, Potter; Studio Manager, Paramount Art District, St. Cloud, Minnesota

Barbara Zaverhue, Fall 1999–ongoing, Apprentice, Roseville, Minnesota

+ John Sullivan, Summer 2000, Potter; Middle School Teacher, Austin, Minnesota

+ Yamaki Shumpei, Spring 2001–ongoing, Apprentice, Kamakura, Japan

Visiting Artists

Kakutani Mitsuo, 1981, 1982, 1995, 1996, 1997, 1998, 1999, and 2000, Painter and Potter; Artist-in-Residence, Earlham College, Richmond, Indiana

Chuck Hindes, 1981, 1996, and 1998, Potter; Professor, School of Art and Art History, University of Iowa, Iowa City, Iowa

Kaneko Jun, 1982, Sculptor, Omaha, Nebraska

* Catherine Mulligan, 1983 and 1997, Sculptor and Teacher, Boulder, Colorado

* James Fritz, 1983, Potter and Teacher, Walla Walla, Washington

* Michael Gwost, 1983, Sculptor, Anacortes, Washington

* Frank Pitcher, 1984, Potter; Assistant Director, Haystack Mountain School of Crafts, Deer Isle, Maine

* John Running-Johnson, 1984, Sculptor; Instructor, Art Department, Western Michigan University, Kalamazoo, Michigan

* David Alban, 1985, Sculptor and Teacher, Cleveland, Ohio

* James A. Jones, 1985, Sculptor; Instructor in Ceramics and Sculpture, Clatsop Community College, Astoria, Oregon

✦ Kimura Kada, Summer 1985–Summer 1986, Potter, Tamataki, Mie Prefecture, Japan

✦ Kimura Akemi, Summer 1985–Summer 1986, Potter, Tamataki, Mie Prefecture, Japan

* James Loftus, 1986, Painter, Plymouth, Massachusetts

* Megan Sweeney, 1986, Sculptor and Teacher, Cleveland, Ohio

* Julie Ravins Byers, 1987, Sculptor, Laytonville, California

* Joseph Samuelson, 1987, Painter and Teacher, Stillwater, Minnesota

* Robin Murphy, 1988, Sculptor; Instructor, Northern Clay Center, Minneapolis, Minnesota

* Sugi Kazuaki, 1985–86, 1988–94, Sculptor, Astoria, New York

* Ada Cruz, 1989, Sculptor, whereabouts unknown

* Sheila Duffy, 1989, Multimedia Artist, Appleton, Wisconsin

* Tadd Jensen, 1989, Sculptor, Little Falls, Minnesota

* Alex Kutchins, 1989, Potter, whereabouts unknown

* Matthew Courtney, 1990, Sculptor, St. Paul, Minnesota

* Anne-Bridget Gary, 1990, Sculptor; Associate Professor of Art and Design, University of Wisconsin, Stevens Point, Wisconsin

* Margaret Breimhurst, 1991, Painter and Textile Artist, St. Paul, Minnesota

* Patricia Marvin, 1991, Painter, Minneapolis, Minnesota

* Mark Gertner, 1998, Sculptor, Minneapolis, Minnesota

* Ann Klefstad, 1998, Sculptor and Editor, Duluth, Minnesota

Koie Ryoji, 1998 and 1999, Potter and Sculptor, Tokoname and Nagura, Aichi Prefecture, Japan

* Annie Baggenstoss, 1999, Sculptor and Teacher, Vermillion, South Dakota

* Jane Frees-Kluth, 1999, Sculptor, Minneapolis, Minnesota

* Jennifer Lorge, 1999, Sculptor, North Branch, Minnesota

* Danielle Callahan, 2000, Environmental Artist, Minneapolis, Minnesota

* Kristin Plucar, 2000, Sculptor, Minneapolis, Minnesota

* Karl Unnasch, 2000, Environmental Artist and Metal Sculptor, Chatfield, Minnesota

* Cynthia Rae Levine, 2001, Sculptor, Minneapolis, Minnesota

Selected Bibliography

Baekeland, Frederick. "Modern Japanese Studio Ceramics and Their Development." In *Modern Japanese Ceramics in American Collections*. New York: Japan Society, 1993.

Barry, Colman J. *Worship and Work: Saint John's Abbey and University, 1856–1980*. Collegeville, Minn.: Order of St. Benedict, 1980.

Becker, Johanna. *Karatsu Ware: A Tradition of Diversity*. Tokyo: Kodansha International, 1986.

Berman, Morris. *The Twilight of American Culture*. New York: W. W. Norton & Co., 2000.

Boyd-Brent, James, and Lindsay Shen. *Here by Design*. St. Paul, Minn.: The Goldstein Museum of Design, 2001.

Bresnahan, Richard. "First Fire." *The Studio Potter* 24, no. 2 (June 1996): 50–53.

———. "Water and Wood Firing." *The Studio Potter* 28, no. 2 (June 2000): 20–22.

Castile, Rand. *The Way of Tea*. New York: John Weatherhill, 1971.

Cort, Louise Allison. "Portrait of a Moment: Japanese Ceramics from 1972 to 1973 in the Weyerhaeuser Collection." In *Shaped with a Passion: The Carl A. Weyerhaeuser Collection of Japanese Ceramics from the 1970s*. Duxbury, Mass.: Art Complex Museum, 1998.

Deutsch, Alfred H. "The Carpenter Shop and Hubert Schneider." In *A Sense of Place II: The Benedictines of Collegeville*. Edited by Colman J. Barry. Collegeville, Minn.: The Liturgical Press, 1990.

Haase, Bill. "Learning to Be an Apprentice." In *Learning in Likely Places: Varieties of Apprenticeship in Japan*. Edited by John Singleton. Cambridge: Cambridge University Press, 1998.

Hauser, Nathanael. *Sacred Art: Beuronese Art at Saint John's*. Collegeville, Minn.: Order of St. Benedict, 1998.

Hunt, William C., ed. "Richard Bresnahan." *Ceramics Monthly* 31, no. 4 (1983): 29–31.

Klassen, John B. "The Rule of Benedict and Environmental Stewardship." Collegeville, Minn., 1998.

Kolb, David A. *Experiential Learning: Experience as the Source of Learning and Development*. Englewood Cliffs, N.J.: Prentice-Hall, 1984.

Leach, Bernard. *Kenzan and His Tradition*. London: Faber and Faber, 1966.

———. *A Potter's Book*. Hollywood-by-the-Sea, Fla.: Transatlantic Arts, 1962.

McLuhan, T. C. *Touch the Earth: A Self-Portrait of Indian Existence*. New York: Promontory Press, 1971.

Nakanodō, Kazunobu. "Japanese Public Collections of Modern Ceramics and Their Direction: From a Museum Curator's Viewpoint." In *Modern Japanese Ceramics in American Collections*. New York: Japan Society, 1993.

New American Bible. Iowa Falls, Iowa: World Bible Publishers, 1970.

Paschke, Jean. "Richard Bresnahan: Stoneware Artisan, Potter, Teacher, Kiln Maker, Environmentalist." *The Crafts Report* (November 1997): 52–54.

Peterson, Susan. *Shōji Hamada: A Potter's Way and Work*. New York: John Weatherhill, 1974.

RB 1980: The Rule of St. Benedict in Latin and English with Notes. Edited by Timothy Fry. Collegeville, Minn.: The Liturgical Press, 1981.

Rhodes, Daniel. *Kilns: Design, Construction, and Operation*. Philadelphia: Chilton Book Co., 1973.

———. *Tamba Pottery: The Timeless Art of a Japanese Village*. Tokyo: Kodansha International, 1975.

Richards, Mary Caroline. *Centering: In Pottery, Poetry, and the Person*. Middletown, Conn.: Wesleyan University Press, 1973. First printing, 1962.

Roloff, Ronald. *Abbey and University Church of Saint John the Baptist*. Revised by Colman Barry. Collegeville, Minn.: Order of St. Benedict, 1980.

Sacred Art at St. John's Abbey. Edited by Wilfred Theisen and Mark Twomey. Collegeville, Minn.: The Liturgical Press, 1980.

Sanders, Herbert H. *The World of Japanese Ceramics*. Tokyo: Kodansha International, 1967.

Scheib, Rebecca. "Cultural Hero Richard Bresnahan: The Art of Life." *Utne Reader* 79 (January 1997): 24.

Singleton, John, ed. *Learning in Likely Places: Varieties of Apprenticeship in Japan*. Cambridge: Cambridge University Press, 1998.

Smith, Barbara F. "Earth Is Alive. I Am Alive." *Ceramics Today— Ryoji Koie* 6 (1984): 9–13.

Tanaka, Sen'ō, and Tanaka Sendō. *The Tea Ceremony*. Tokyo: Kodansha International, 2000.

Welch, Matthew. "Out of the Fire." *Arts Magazine* 19, no. 4 (April 1996): 8–9.

Williams, Gerry, ed. *Apprenticeship in Craft*. Goffstown, N.H.: Daniel Clark Books, 1981.

———. "The Japanese Pottery Tradition and Its Influence on American Ceramics." *American Craft* 58, no. 2 (April 1998): 52–59.

Wilson, Richard. *Inside Japanese Ceramics: A Primer of Materials, Techniques, and Traditions*. New York: John Weatherhill, 1995.

Wright, Malcolm. "A Portfolio of American Wood-Fired Pottery." *The Studio Potter* 11, no. 1 (December 1982): 6–24.

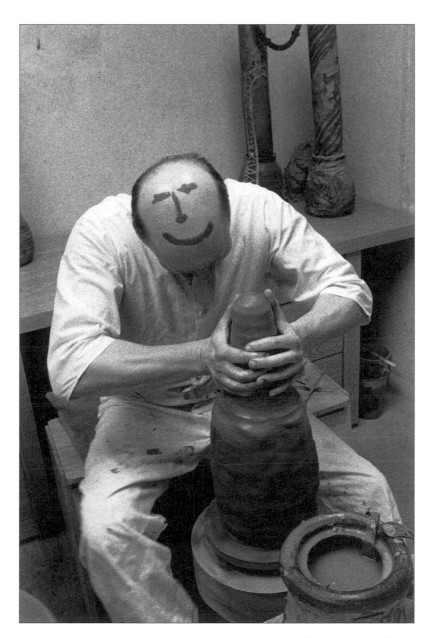

Frustrated by his attempts to get a photograph of Bresnahan's face while he was throwing pots, James Dean picked up a brush loaded with iron slip and painted the top of his friend's head. Dean and Bresnahan laughingly call this image "The Happy Potter."

Photograph by James R. Dean, 1996.

Body of Clay
Soul of Fire

Richard Bresnahan and
the Saint John's Pottery

Edited by Sandra L. Lipshultz

Designed by Barbara J. Arney

Printed on 100 lb. Luna Matte

Typefaces are Garamond
and Optima

Tip-in is Sweet Potato Vine
Japanese paper by Awagami